VELVALEE DICKINSON: The "Doll Woman" Spy

Barbara Casey

Published in the United States of America by:

Strategic Media Books, Inc.
782 Wofford St., Rock Hill, SC 29730
www.strategicmediabooks.com

Manufactured in the United States of America.

ISBN-10: 1-939521-74-2
ISBN-13: 978-1-939521-74-3

Requests for permission should be directed to:
strategicmediabooks@gmail.com

or mailed to:

Permissions
Strategic Media Books, Inc.
782 Wofford St.
Rock Hill, SC 29730

Distributed to the trade by:

Cardinal Publishers Group
2402 North Shadeland Ave., Suite A
Indianapolis, IN 46219

DISCLAIMERS

The information presented in this book is based on federal and state court records and files, FBI memoranda and documents, secret service files, police records, and information in the media. All reasonable efforts have been made to credit sources and present the facts truthfully and coherently.

***

All of the quotations in this book are written as they appeared in the original source. No attempt has been made to correct spelling or punctuation.

***

OTHER BOOKS BY BARBARA CASEY

Nonfiction

Kathryn Kelly: The Moll behind Machine Gun Kelly

Assata Shakur: A 20th Century Escaped Slave

Fiction

The Gospel According to Prissy

The Cadence of Gypsies (Book 1 of The F.I.G. Mysteries)

The Wish Rider (Book 2 of The F.I.G. Mysteries)

The Clock Flower (Book 3 of The F.I.G. Mysteries)

The Nightjar's Promise (Book 4 of The F.I.G. Mysteries)

The House of Kane

The Coach's Wife

Shyla's Initiative

Just Like Family

Charlotte Woods

Carla Harward

Rene Mathews

Sophia Harward

The beautiful women in my life

who fill me

with love and inspiration

Table of Contents

Prologue

A nation can survive its fools, and even the ambitious. But it cannot survive treason from within. An enemy at the gates is less formidable, for he is known and carries his banner openly. But the traitor moves amongst those within the gate freely, his sly whispers rustling through all the alleys, heard in the very halls of government itself.

Marcus Tullius Cicero

Small-boned, petite—no more than 5 feet tall, if that, and weighing less than 100 pounds, Velvalee Malvena Dickinson hurried into the Midtown Manhattan bank. She feared that the FBI was watching her, and her immediate mission was to remove the contents of her safety deposit box in case she needed to make a quick escape.

She was too late, however.

In fact, the FBI had been surveilling Velvalee for well over a year. They now had enough evidence for an arrest on the suspicion of violating wartime censorship codes, at the very least, and possibly espionage, which, if convicted, carried the death penalty.

As soon as she opened the metal box, FBI agents who had followed her into the dimly-lit vault announced that she was under arrest. When she flung the box at the agents, they immediately confiscated its contents which included $15,940, two-thirds of it in Federal Reserve Notes that were later traced through their serial numbers to the Japanese Consulate.

These same bills had been withdrawn by the Imperial Japanese Government before the bombing of Pearl Harbor. Immediately prior to being transferred to Velvalee, they had been in the possession of Captain Yuzo Ishikawa of the Japanese Naval Inspector's Office in New York. Also discovered in the safety deposit box were secret Japanese codes and instructions on the use of them.

ꕥ ✵ ꕥ

Chapter 1

The Beginnings

Velvalee Malvena Blucher was born October 12, 1893, in Sacramento, California. Of German descent, her father was Otto Blucher (aka Bluehar) who was originally from Virginia. He died in 1923 after getting crushed in a car wheel at the age of 61. Velvalee's mother was Elizabeth Carlton Blucher, the former Elizabeth Carlton Bottoms, originally from Kentucky and also of German descent. She died at the age of 46 from tuberculosis in 1919.

Both of Velvalee's parents are buried in Sacramento's Historic City Cemetery. Established in 1849, it is one of the oldest existing cemeteries in

Sacramento and tasked with preserving California history since the Gold Rush era. Velvalee had a brother eleven years her junior, Oswald Otto (Ossie) Blucher, born in 1900 also in Sacramento. The only other family on record is a Mrs. Malvina Blucher who died at the age of 64 in 1894. Possibly the grandmother of Velvalee on her paternal side, she is buried in the same plat B128, Lot 24, as Velvalee's parents at the beautiful Historic City Cemetery in a lush garden setting.

Velvalee graduated from the Sacramento High School and studied Japanese for a while at a private seminary in Berkeley. After finding it too difficult, she started classes at Sacramento Junior College and later the University of California, eventually graduating in 1928 from Leland Stanford Junior University, colloquially known as "the Farm." It wasn't until nineteen years later, in January 1937, that she received her Bachelor of Arts degree, however, allegedly because she had not returned books owned by the university. She would claim years later that she was traveling at the time of her graduation and unable to attend the ceremony, which was the reason for the delay in receiving her degree.

In the mid-1920s, Velvalee was employed in a San Francisco bank during which time she married twice, both marriages ending in divorce. Then from 1928 through 1935, she worked as a bookkeeper at a San Francisco produce commodity brokerage company in California's Imperial Valley.

Owned by her future husband, Lee Taylor Dickinson, the firm had many Japanese clients, so it was not surprising that the couple became active in the Japanese-American Society. Founded in 1909, the stated purpose of the Society, which continues today, was to build economic, cultural, governmental and personal relationships between the people of Japan and America. However, "shady dealings," as described by the FBI, possibly because of the stigma attached with the Dickinsons' close association with the Japanese, caused the brokerage company to be closed. This resulted in the Dickinsons losing their membership in the Society, only to be reinstated by a Japanese diplomat, Kaoru Nakashima, who underwrote their Society dues.

Shortly after her marriage to Lee, Velvalee became involved in social services. Her employment with the California State Emergency Relief Administration in San Francisco, and with the County Welfare Department as a social services investigator in the Southern California area until 1937 also brought her into close contact with the Japanese community, the Niseis.

It was during this time, the FBI would later determine, that Velvalee made numerous visits to the Japanese Consulate as well as the Japanese Institute, an organization designed to "preserve and promote the awareness of and the appreciation for Japanese language and culture." In addition, she attended important social gatherings at which Japanese Navy members and other highly ranked Japanese government officials were present. She was frequently entertained by Japanese dignitaries and invited on Japanese warships, and on numerous occasions Velvalee and her husband invited many Japanese people they knew into their home as guests.

Velvalee often dressed in authentic Japanese attire at these various occasions, and it has been reported that her name was in a book brought to the United States from Japan by a Japanese spy. In addition, Velvalee had a wide-ranging collection of Japanese musical recordings as well as an extensive library of books about Japanese customs and beliefs, art and music that included such titles as *Bushido, The Romance of Japan,* and *Japanese Traits and Foreign Influence.* Many of her books had been personally inscribed to Velvalee by the Japanese authors. She also had Japanese jewelry and silver, and Japanese pictures.

This interest and familiarity in the Japanese and their connections within the *Niseis*, however, made it increasingly difficult for Velvalee and Lee to succeed professionally because of the mounting negative sentiment against the Japanese. They became referred to by the people they associated with who were not Japanese as "Jap lovers," a pejorative term which was becoming more prevalent as the threat of war took on the appearance of reality and not just idle gossip.

Velvalee began collecting dolls in 1934 at the age of 41 when a friend gave her a pair of native dolls from the Philippines. As other friends began giving Velvalee dolls, her interest in collecting dolls grew. In 1937, she and her husband borrowed 100 dollars from a friend and moved to New York City where they took rooms in the Hotel Peter Stuyvesant on Manhattan's West 86th Street, not too far from Washington Square. With Lee's health in serious decline, complicated further by his love of alcoholic beverages, Velvalee began working as a sales clerk in Bloomingdale's doll department over the holiday season, successfully selling the dolls and earning eighteen dollars a week.

According to doll historian Loretta Nardone, costume doll collecting was then a burgeoning pastime supported by local clubs, specialty dealers, and avid hobbyists. Distinctly an adult activity, primarily women collected dolls for their beauty, for associations, and for memories they invoked of dolls they had in their own childhood. These same reasons for collecting dolls continue today, which makes it one of the largest hobby groups in the world.

Velvalee continued to build up her collection, acquiring an array of foreign, antique, and rare dolls. Confiding she was "tired of accepting orders from others," she started publishing a list of her dolls that were for sale as early as 1939, and she joined the Doll Collectors of America with its headquarters in Ft. Edward, New York. She also became a member of the Toy Collectors Club of New York, the parent company of the United Federation of Doll Clubs (UFDC). However, after passing a resolution in September 1944 that its members had to be "true 100 percent American," the UFDC removed Velvalee from its membership roster a month later.

Soon after moving to New York, Velvalee was elected to membership in the Japanese Institute of New York and was a frequent caller at the Nippon Club where she appeared wearing traditional Japanese attire and sipped diluted sake or tea. This was a private social club founded in 1905 by chemist Jokichi Takamine for Japanese Americans and Japanese nationals.

There were also other women who visited there, even though it had originally been established as a "gentlemen's club," patterned after the all-men's clubs in England. Included among Velvalee's many Japanese friends were Kaname Wakasugi, the Japanese consul general, and Ichira Yokoyama, the naval attaché at the embassy in Washington, DC.

For a time, Velvalee and her husband lived with her brother, Oswald, in a co-op apartment. Early the following year she opened her own doll shop specializing in rare and antique dolls, first out of the apartment at 680 Madison Avenue, and eventually in October 1941, she moved her business to the fashionable and spacious storefront located at 718 Madison Avenue. The Dickinsons and their live-in maid resided nearby on Madison Avenue between 61st and 62nd Street.

The Valvalee Dickinson doll shop catered to collectors throughout the United States and overseas who were interested in foreign, regional, and antique dolls. Her clientele, which eventually numbered up to 20,000, included movie and Broadway stars, assorted social celebrities, as well as affluent men and women of the carriage trade. The prices she charged these collectors for her highly sought-after dolls started at a minimum of twenty-five dollars, with some of the more rare dolls fetching well into the thousands of dollars.

She also worked hard to make dolls available at lower prices for her more pedestrian, less prosperous customers. In a large ad she placed in *Doll News*, the official newsletter of the National Doll and Toy Collectors of New York, she advertised 7-inch cloth dolls from Palestine at five dollars for a group of three; Japanese *ichimatsu* dolls from 10 to 14 inches at ten dollars to eighteen dollars; Chad Valley royal children dolls, 15 to 18 inches for ten dollars to fifteen dollars; and a preprinted cloth doll pattern for one dollar.

An aggressive and creative marketer, Velvalee wrote several articles for *The Complete Collector*, a specialized journal for antique collectors. The somewhat lengthy, florid subtitle for these articles was "A Monthly Discourse on the Fine Arts for the Contemplative Man's Recreation."

It was primarily through Velvalee's frequent correspondence with clients and other doll collectors that gave her doll store the most notice, however. All of her letters, note cards, and other stationery were written on customized blue stationery embellished with a scarlet border and letterhead advertising her business in "Dolls – Antique – Foreign – Regional – Playthings." The brochures she mailed out, written on the same customized blue stationery, were also embellished with a scarlet letterhead and a border of international dolls which boasted: "We have dolls from nearly every country in the world and state in the United States."

Oswald Dickinson moved in with his sister and brother-in-law in 1942 and assisted Velvalee in her store occasionally. Previously employed at Western Electric in Brooklyn, he had also been a labor analyst in San Francisco, and had worked for the Labor Relations War Production Board in Washington, DC.

And even though he was in poor health and suffering from Bright's disease which caused a serious heart ailment, Lee Dickinson, Velvalee's husband, took care of the accounting and business transactions for the doll shop, including those involving the sale of dolls to influential, wealthy individuals throughout the United States and abroad.

There was a great deal of interest in the Velvalee Dickinson doll shop, which attractively displayed her vast collection of the latest dolls from Paris and England, as well as other parts of the world, particularly since at that time the import of foreign dolls of all types had been cut off due to the war. There is a record, in fact, that one of her purchases, from Howard F. Porter of the Old Print Exchange, New York City, was four early wax dolls made about 1770 and presented in 1808 to Mary Dance, the famous British actress. These valuable dolls, which represent a clergyman and wife, and a soldier and wife, are made of yellow and pink wax over wood, and previously had been sold to Howard Porter by Mary Dance's descendants.

Another doll that was part of Velvalee's extensive collection was the Adelina Patti character doll. Patterned after the world-famous opera singer who was born in Madrid, Spain, in 1843, the Adelina Patti china shoulder head doll was created at the Alt, Beck, and Gottschalk porcelain factories of Nauendorg, Germany in the early 1880s. Simon and Halbig, based in Thuringen, Germany, fashioned the doll with authentic antique earrings and necklace, and a beautiful velvet and antique lace gown, making the doll quite valuable. This doll eventually found its way into the collection of Mrs. Hazel Leland, grandmother of fourteen grandchildren.

Always in the market to build up her extensive, eclectic high-quality inventory, in February 1940, Velvalee bought the rare Charles Jopp dolls to add to her own valuable collection. A month later, an article appeared in the *Science Christian Monitor* publicizing that the dolls were for sale:

When Dolldom Goes on Parade

A Part of the Rare Charles Jopp Collection

Walking dolls, nursemaid, boy bicycler, fashionable ladies - belonging in collection once owned by Charles Jopp, Danvers, Massachusetts, now by Mrs. Velvalee Dickinson of New York City

The Velvalee Dickinson doll store also had a few detractors, however. Doll collector, Mrs. Fred Mason of Chicago, would describe visiting the Madison Avenue store, "I didn't like the shop.... It seemed sinister, although of course I didn't know the owner was a spy."

It was through Velvalee's correspondence, frequent advertising, and lectures around the country that she made a name for herself as an expert in rare dolls. She exhibited her dolls in prestigious antique shows, and one doll in particular, an 18th century wooden doll, was mentioned in *The New York Times* in 1940. Her opinion was sought and respected on all doll subjects, and her frequent travels across the United States were treated as news worthy in newspapers and magazines because of her celebrity status.

In spite of her growing recognition in the doll world, however, the doll business was limited and, therefore, not a great financial success. Lee's constant medical problems continued to worsen and drain their monetary resources. The lingering after effects of the Great Depression continued to dictate the spending habits of Americans more toward necessities. The fear of financial instability brought on by the war caused uncertainty.

Frustrated, Velvalee sent letters to her customers complaining that the war was causing hardships and she was having a difficult time procuring dolls from overseas. In early January 1940, she wrote:

> *...Native dolls are becoming very very rare; in fact, in some countries Dolls are no more. Doll materials are now being used in the manufacture of war munitions. I have made every effort to obtain Dolls from countries now in the war zones, especially those countries that we know have discontinued manufacturing Dolls....*

There was also an incident reported in a 1944 edition of *St. Louis Sunday Morning* that on November 26, 1941, a few days before the bombing of Pearl Harbor, a witness observed a "well-dressed Japanese naval officer dart through the door" of the doll shop and "hand a small, compact bundle to the proprietor" whispering he might not be able to come again. When Velvalee suggested that they might meet in Honolulu, a place she might like to live, he emphatically exclaimed, "No! Not Honolulu!" The FBI would later determine that the bundle contained $25,000.

In addition, when civilian travel had been brought practically to a standstill because of the war, there were lengthy and expensive trips made by the Dickinsons to California involving stops in Washington and Oregon and other places for the purpose of "business, pleasure, and health."

ೞ ✵ ೞ

Chapter 2

The Suspicions

These were strange, confusing, and difficult times for the United States. Across the Atlantic in Europe, a power-hungry Adolph Hitler had declared himself "Fuhrer" and was determined to build an empire—the Third Reich. With Germany already under his control, he proceeded to annex Austria and the Sudetenland, a German-speaking region in Czechoslovakia. Then in 1939, Hitler seized the rest of Czechoslovakia and invaded Poland. As a result, England and France declared war.

In the Far East, Japan was making military waves as well. The Japanese Imperial Army invaded China in

1937, seized its northern capital Peiping, which was later named Beijing, began taking control of coastal areas and nearby islands dotting the Pacific, and deliberately sank an American gunboat, the USS Panay (PR-5), while it was anchored in the Yangtze River outside Nanking (now spelled Nanjing), China. It formally joined with Hitler's Germany and Mussolini's Italy to form the Axis powers in September 1940 in an effort to secure their own specific expansionist interests.

Protected by two oceans, an isolationist America was determined to remain neutral. However, the lingering Great Depression provided the impetus for tyranny and despotism. Groups like the German American Bund and the Silver Shirts embraced the Fascist and Nazi movements, and many Americans were increasingly becoming attracted to the promise of a classless state.

In the early 1930s, the Federal Bureau of Investigation (FBI) had faced primarily homegrown gun-slinging gangsters—from "Scarface" and "Baby Face" to Ma Barker and Kathryn Kelly, "Machine Gun" Kelly's moll. Now, however, as they approached the end of the decade, a new type of villain was threatening, primarily from afar. Fascist dictators, fanatical militarists, and revolution-exporting communists seemed to be ubiquitous across the globe, along with their legions of spies, saboteurs, and subversive agents—whose mission was to invade, infiltrate, or even conquer. They threatened the fate of people and nations, and the survival of democracy itself.

In an effort to protect the United States from these suspected groups that were crossing U.S. borders and breaking lines into criminal activity, in 1936 President Franklin Roosevelt and Secretary of State Cordell Hull tasked the Federal Bureau of Investigation with gathering intelligence on the potential threats to national security posed specifically by fascist and communist groups. In addition, because the intelligence arms of the Army and Navy had noticed increased activity by German and Japanese spies in the late 1930s, they began working cohesively with the Bureau to disrupt it.

With the start of a new decade, the nation was drifting towards war and was increasingly supporting the Allied cause. In charge of domestic intelligence, the Bureau had already built an extensive network of sources, with law enforcement around the country serving as an important set of eyes and ears. It had also been developing connections abroad with Canadian and British intelligence and law enforcement.

In 1940 Roosevelt decided to assign intelligence responsibilities for different parts of the globe to various agencies. The Bureau was assigned the Western Hemisphere, and FBI agents vigorously began working undercover in Central and South America as part of the Bureau's "Special Intelligence Service" (later to become the CIA) in response to Roosevelt's order.

By this time, South America had become a hotbed of German intrigue and a staging ground for the Nazis to send spies into the United States. With more than half-a-million German emigrants—many supporters of the Third Reich—settled in Brazil and Argentina alone, it was fast becoming a hub for relaying information back to Germany. When the United States joined the Allied cause in 1941, Roosevelt was determined to keep an eye on the Nazi activities of our neighbors to the south in order to protect the nation from Hitler's spies and collect intelligence to help win the war.

Over the next seven years, the FBI sent more than three hundred and forty agents and support professionals undercover, including cryptologists who specialized in code breaking, into Central and South America as part of the Special Intelligence Service. During that time, the undercover operatives mastered the language, learned the culture, and gathered information to send back to J. Edgar Hoover's FBI Headquarters in Washington, DC. That information was then crafted into useful intelligence for the military and others.

The FBI also started officially stationing agents as diplomatic liaisons in U.S. embassies—the forerunner of today's Legal Attachés—to coordinate international leads arising from the Bureau's work. Overseas, it developed ways of sharing crucial information with law enforcement and intelligence services there in order to capture Axis spies and saboteurs.

The Bureau's domestic counterintelligence work continued full force as well. The FBI employed a variety of double agents to disrupt enemy espionage, set up radio networks to gather intelligence and spread disinformation, and used its growing scientific and technological capabilities to track down spies, home grown or otherwise.

When war finally did come to America with the Japanese bombing of Pearl Harbor on a quiet Sunday, at 7:55 am, December 7, 1941, the Bureau was prepared. As the bombs fell, Honolulu Special Agent in Charge Robert Shivers was on the phone with FBI Headquarters and

Director J. Edgar Hoover, who immediately implemented the war plans the FBI already had in place and put the organization on a 24/7 schedule.

Tennessee native Shivers had been handpicked by Director Hoover to run the Honolulu office precisely because of his leadership skills. Shivers was minted as a special agent in 1920, and after serving across the South and Midwest and in New York, Shivers was tapped to lead field offices in Pittsburgh, Buffalo, and Miami. However, because of nagging health issues, he went on restricted duty in the late 1930s.

In the summer of 1939, with Europe on the verge of war, and the U.S. supporting the Allied cause, Hoover once again turned to Shivers to re-open the now strategically important FBI division in Honolulu. Within a few months, Shivers, described as smart and genteel, developed strong relationships with local police as well as with Army and Navy forces, and he also began making contacts in the islands' Japanese communities. These deepened when he and his wife began caring for a Japanese schoolgirl named Shizue Kobatake. It was her responsibility to do light housekeeping for the Shrivers, and they, in turn, provided a home for Shizue. Within a short time after moving in with the Shrivers, she legally changed her name to Suzanne Kobatake and became a U.S. Citizen.

Immediately following the attack on Pearl Harbor, Shivers placed the Japanese Consulate under police guard, both to protect the diplomats from retaliation and to prevent their escape. Also at that time, his agents seized a large quantity of suspiciously coded documents that consulate employees tried to hastily burn and began running down key cases of espionage.

Another major issue involved the one hundred fifty thousand people of Japanese ancestry in Hawaii—roughly a third of the population. Some argued that they should be taken into custody. Shivers and key members of the armed services, along with the territorial government, strongly disagreed, however, and this decision made a vital difference in preventing the kind of mass internment that happened on the U.S. mainland. As a result, only a few thousand Japanese nationals considered a security risk ended up being detained.

Shivers soon gained respect across the islands, earning significant authority from its military governor. Even though his health forced him to retire in 1943, Shivers was later lauded by the territorial Senate of Hawaii both for "safeguarding Hawaii's internal security" and for displaying "sympathy, sound judgment, and firmness."

ꕥ ✵ ꕥ

Chapter 3

The Letters

As the country absorbed the shock of the bombing at Pearl Harbor and tried to adjust to the new and difficult reality of rationing and travel restrictions while tearfully watching their loved ones depart for war zones in places unknown, the "Doll Woman," Velvalee Dickinson, continued sending out her chatty, gossipy correspondence to her clientele and other doll enthusiasts.

One letter about dolls, however, posted from New York and sent to Señora Ines de Molinali in Argentina, was intercepted by wartime censors because of its unusual and somewhat confusing contents, as well as incorrect postage. The letter, dated January 27, 1942, was brought to the Bureau's attention in February 1942. Purportedly written by Maud Bowman of Portland, Oregon, the letter mentioned a "wonderful doll hospital" where the writer had left her three "Old English dolls" for repairs. Also mentioned in the letter were "fishing nets" and "balloons."

If dolls were somehow being used to assist the enemy, it wouldn't be the first time. During the American Civil War, contraband, medical supplies, and messages were smuggled across the Northern lines inside the hollow interiors of dolls carried in the protective arms of little girls. More recently, smugglers from the United States concealed amphetamines inside small, soft "Minion" dolls and shipped them to Israel.

FBI cryptographers, and in particular C.A. Appel, examined the letter and eventually concluded that it was likely the "dolls" in question were possibly three warships and the "doll hospital" was a West Coast-based shipyard where repairs were made. They also speculated that the "fishing nets" referred to an aircraft carrier with antitorpedo netting on its sides, the "wooden doll" was an older battleship, and the "little boy" was a destroyer. "Balloons" mentioned in the letter probably disclosed information about coastal defenses and other critical information on the West Coast.

During the first half of 1942 it appears that Velvalee along with her husband remained on the move. They traveled first to Seattle, then to San Francisco, and back to New York in March. She reopened her store for several days and then returned to Seattle, with a stop in Portland. The Dickinsons continued their journey south to Oakland, California, and after a brief stay there, traveled possibly into Mexico briefly where they purchased hand-crafted dolls, then through the southern part of the United States before returning to New York.

These trips couldn't have been easy. They also had to be extremely expensive. With the United States now involved in the war, gasoline rationing was in place thereby making automobile travel virtually impossible. Travel by train was equally difficult. Crowded waiting rooms at railroad stations, military troop trains receiving green light priority on all lines, servicemen on furlough commandeering what little space was available on regular passenger trains, and food rationing in place; yet Velvalee and Lee, even in declining health, somehow managed. For any of their more extended visits in an area, they stayed in hotels, and while in the San Francisco area, they relied on a realtor who handled Lee Dickinson's property interests, Henry Jeffs, to chauffeur them around. The Dickinson property consisted of the North Hotel in Seattle, Washington, that had been left to Lee by his late uncle, John Godwin. Jeffs would later state in an FBI interview that Velvalee impressed him "as a very self-centered and selfish woman of an extremely grasping nature. She was primarily concerned with how much she could get out of the real estate which comprised the Dickinson estate."

It was also in early 1942 when Mrs. Mary Wallace from Springfield, Ohio, about thirteen hours by train from New York, received a letter returned to her from Argentina and stamped by the postal service in Buenos Aires. It was in a red, blue, and white envelope, and like the first letter that had been intercepted, this letter had been addressed to a Señora Ines Lopez de Molinali, 2563 O'Higgins Street, Buenos Aires, Argentina. The return address correctly showed Mary Wallace's address of 1808 High Street, Springfield, Ohio.

There were many similarities to the first letter. The information on the envelope was typewritten, and in addition to the Argentine stamp, there was an American stamp of the Central Station of New York and dated the month before. A separate stamp revealed the words, roughly translated from Spanish to English: "Recipient party without leaving the forwarding address rejected to the sender."

When Mrs. Wallace opened the letter and read it, it almost appeared as though it had been written by someone illiterate. There were numerous typographical errors, misspellings, incorrect grammar, and many inconsistencies, yet some things did reveal certain personal happenings in her life, such as her nephew's serious illness. Totally confused and wondering if it might be someone's idea of a bad joke, Mrs. Wallace gave the letter, later to become known as "the Springfield letter," to the Director at the Springfield Post Office who in turn sent it to the FBI in Washington where the letter was carefully studied. A short time later, Mrs. Wallace was called in for questioning.

The agent who questioned Mary Wallace, known only as Agent B, was particularly interested in what Mrs. Wallace told him about her doll collection, her activities with the Springfield Art Circle, and how she had recently purchased several dolls from a Madison Avenue shop in New York. She also described to the agent how kind Mrs. Dickinson, the owner of the shop, had been, especially since they both were experiencing tragedy—Mrs.

Dickinson's late husband's death and her own nephew's incurable brain tumor.

The contents of the letter were simply too strange to be innocent and too vague to be a joke. The postal censorship authorities had almost let the original letter they had intercepted pass, thinking that the letter writer was just a little addled. However, with the second letter now being returned, Agent B had a different theory, one which he shared with the FBI cryptologists.

This crucial second letter had been sent to the same address in Argentina as the first letter that had been intercepted by the censors and returned to an address of the person who supposedly wrote it but had no knowledge of it. Like the first letter, it also discussed dolls:

> *You asked me to tell you about my collection a month ago. I had to give a talk to an art club, so I talked about my dolls and figurines. The only new dolls I have are THREE LOVELY IRISH dolls. One of these three dolls is an old Fisherman with a Net over his back – another is an old woman with wood on her back and the third is a little boy. Everyone seemed to enjoy my talk. I can only think of our sick boy these days. You wrote me that you had sent a letter to Mr. Shaw, well I want to see MR. SHAW he distroyed Your letter, you know he has been Ill. His car was damaged but is being repaired now. I saw a few of his family*

about. They all say Mr. Shaw will be back to work soon.

Mrs. Wallace who turned over the letter said the signature looked somewhat like hers, and the writer seemed to know quite a bit about her personal life and of her interest in dolls, but she had not sent it. The return address was correctly noted on the envelope as an Ohio address, but the letter had been postmarked New York, a place where Mrs. Wallace had not been when the letter was mailed, her main source of entertainment being the Springfield Art Circle in the town where she lived. Besides that, she didn't know how to type and didn't care to learn.

In the letter, the FBI focused their attention on the reference to "Mr. Shaw." In early 1942, the Japanese needed to know how badly the American Pacific fleet had been damaged in the Pearl Harbor attack on December 7, 1941, and how quickly the United States Navy was making repairs.

USS *Shaw* (DD-373) was a *Mahan* class destroyer commissioned in 1936, and fully operational in 1938. After training in the Atlantic, she was transferred to the

Pacific where she conducted various exercises and provided services to carriers and submarines operating in the area. By mid-February 1941, *Shaw* entered the Navy Yard at Pearl Harbor_for repairs, dry docking in YFD-2.

On December 7, *Shaw* was still dry docked, receiving adjustments to her depth charge mechanisms. During the Japanese attack, she took three hits—two bombs through the forward machine gun platform, and one through the port wing of the bridge. Fires spread rapidly through the ship. By 9:25 that morning, all fire-fighting facilities were exhausted, and the order to abandon ship was given. Efforts to flood the dock were only partially successful, and shortly after 9:30 am, her forward magazine exploded.

When the Japanese attacked Pearl Harbor, the crew of the *Shaw* was ashore, "as was customary for vessels undergoing overhaul in dry dock, and only a few men were on hand when the bombs started to fall," according to *U.S. Destroyer Operations in WW II*. Even so, USS *Shaw* lost twenty-four crewmen during the attack.

Temporary repairs were made at Pearl Harbor during December 1941 and January 1942. Then, on February 9, *Shaw* steamed towards San Francisco, about two weeks before the Springfield letter was sent, where repairs were completed, including the installation of a new bow.

Noticing the incorrect spelling of "distroyed" and the word "Your" capitalized immediately following—possibly indicating the word "destroyer," the FBI concluded that the letter's information tied in with the USS *Shaw*, damaged in the Pearl Harbor attack. With repairs now being completed on the West Coast, it would soon be part of the Pacific fleet once again.

While being questioned by the FBI, Mrs. Wallace also gave the agents all the correspondence she had received from other fellow doll collectors over the years. One letter to her, the FBI forensics determined, had been typed on the same typewriter, a portable Underwood #621465, used to write the coded letter. It had been sent by Velvalee Dickinson, who owned an upscale shop at 718 Madison Avenue in New York that specialized in collectible and antique dolls. As they gathered information, the agents continued to observe the activities of Mary Wallace and her husband, as well as interview their friends and family.

Then, a short time later, in August 1942, a third letter was turned over to the FBI, supposedly written by Sara Gellert of Portland, Oregon, and postmarked Oakland, California. Written in early February, it had been returned to the woman who was also a doll collector but who had no knowledge of having written the letter.

The letter mentioned her little grandson "staying in bed only if he could play with his father's fishing nets while the little girl demands balloons." The letter went on to say:

> *You know I have three old China head dolls from England. I do not like these dolls. However, my dear husband bought them for me. It will take this Doll hospital a few months before they will have them completely repaired, then will send. There is so much repair work to do, new parts needed as arms and legs....*

The FBI cryptographers concluded that the three China head dolls were battleships being repaired near Central California after being damaged in Honolulu. After getting an update from the United States Naval authorities on their fleet—condition and location—FBI cryptographers deciphered this to mean that the writer had secured information on an aircraft carrier warship—the USS *Saratoga.*

USS *Saratoga* (CV-3) was a *Lexington*-class aircraft carrier built for the United States Navy during the 1920s. Originally designed as a battlecruiser, she was converted into one of the Navy's first aircraft carriers during construction to comply with the Washington Naval Treaty of 1922. The ship entered service in 1928 and was assigned to the Pacific Fleet for her entire career.

After being torpedoed and suffering major damages in the Pacific, *Saratoga* had been undergoing repairs in Puget Sound Naval Shipyard in Bremerton, Washington. When the Japanese attacked Pearl Harbor on December 7, 1941, *Saratoga* had already been repaired, and was waiting for a plain warship to be converted into a second aircraft carrier that would join her in the Pacific.

This letter mailed from Portland, Oregon, had been written a few days after the aircraft carrier USS *Saratoga* left Puget Sound for San Diego Harbor to embark her air group, which had been training ashore while the ship was refitting.

The Oregon doll collector who had received the returned letter was a physician's wife, a frail little woman—a semi-invalid. The letter she had supposedly written mentioned that since it was "getting on to the first of the month" she would need to get busy "sending out my husband's monthly statements." But, in fact, this woman didn't send out the monthly billing statements for her husband and never had; he always hired someone to do that.

A second letter supposedly written by Sara Gellert was also turned over to the FBI in August 1942. Dated May 20, 1942, in this letter the name of the doll collector's daughter mentioned was incorrect, but the fact that her daughter's bedroom was now vacant since her marriage was accurate and something she had mentioned to a fellow doll collector, Velvalee Dickinson. And, in fact, she had even invited Mrs. Dickinson and her husband to use the room if ever they were in Portland after Velvalee had complained to her about finding adequate places to stay when traveling. The letter read in part:

> *I just secured a lovely Siamese Temple Dancer, it had been damaged, that is tore in the middle. But it is now repaired, and I like it very much. I could not get a mate for this Siam dancer, so I am*

> *redressing just a small plan ordinary doll into a second Siam doll...*

Suspicions were clearly mounting when still another letter, the fifth, was turned over to the FBI by a Colorado Springs, Colorado, woman in August 1942. Supposedly written by recently divorced Freda Maytag, this letter, dated February 1942, carried a Seattle, Washington, postmark and referred to "five English dolls which I am shipping home as a Christmas surprise," suggesting five battleships in complete condition at that time.

She also wrote about making Chinese dolls for her daughter. It had been written shortly after a convoy of ships arrived at the Mare Island Naval Shipyard, located 25 miles northeast of San Francisco in Vallejo, California. According to the FBI, further details of the ships were clearly included in the letter using terms as though describing the dolls, but, in fact, were giving information on the convoy.

> *...I purchased seven small dolls which in a short time I hope and expect to make look as if they were real seven Chinese dolls....I have almost finished the mother doll. I will then make a*

Chinese father, grandfather, grandmother and three children....The children will be girl, boy, and baby.

Once again, a check by the FBI with naval authorities verified their conclusions that the dolls referred to were seven small boats being converted into aircraft carriers.

In the same letter, there was mention that the letter writer, Freda Maytag, was planning to spend a week in Seattle with her son who would join her there on business. When questioned by the agents, Freda Maytag remembered telling a New York doll dealer who was also staying in the Seattle hotel at the time about her son.

Just like the other letters, this long, typewritten letter was also addressed to a woman in South America the collector had never heard of, yet it had her signature.

At first glance, Velvalee's letters looked innocent enough, but the FBI quickly figured out that the reference to "Irish Dolls" and old women with packs on their backs actually meant modern aircraft carriers, and that "the cute little doll shop" she happened to run across where "they did repairs so skillfully" was not a reference to the well-known Humpty Dumpty Hospital run by Emma C. Clear and her husband, Wallace, in Redondo Beach, California, but was in fact a report on the condition of the battleships bombed in Pearl Harbor.

From January 1942 until August 1942—the same time the Dickinsons had been traveling to the West Coast and then back to New York by way of the southern states, a total of five letters surfaced, from four different correspondents and all, except for Mrs. Mary Wallace, living west of the Rockies. It was during this period when the entire world seemed to be at war, and spies on all sides were most active. Often the people who appeared most unlikely of being spies were, drawn into the dangerous activity because of money, the excitement, and not always understanding the enormous negative ramifications of their actions.

What FBI agents quickly learned from their counterparts stationed in South America was that the woman all of the letters had been addressed to in Buenos Aires — Señora Ines Lopez de Molinali, 2563 O'Higgins Street, Buenos Aires, Argentina—had already been picked up on suspicion of being a spy. Unknown to Velvalee, when she wrote the letters, her contact in Buenos Aires was no longer there to receive them. Therefore, the letters had been returned.

If any letters had reached the South America address before the FBI became suspicious, certainly none did from that time on. Postal censor authorities had been alerted by the FBI around the country as well as in South America—particularly Argentina—to be on the lookout for any letters that discussed dolls or packages containing dolls.

The five letters had been mailed in various cities and signed with the names of well-known doll collectors, all of whom were members of highly respected American families with unsullied reputations for patriotism going back for generations. Nevertheless, in an abundance of caution and thoroughness, for a year the federal agents shadowed each of these families who had supposedly written the letters and had them returned. Much to the chagrin of these five women who shared a passion for dolls, the FBI also investigated their relatives, friends and all their contacts, but without result.

One contact did prove especially helpful, however. Mr. and Mrs. Wallace C. Clear of Los Angeles, California, were well-known experts in the doll world.

Mrs. Emma Clear was the founder and "head surgeon" of Humpty Dumpty Doll Hospital, originating in Buffalo, New York, in 1908, moving to Cleveland in 1914, and finally settling in Redondo Beach, California in 1917. It was here that "Mama" and "Papa" Clear, as they were affectionately called, repaired dolls and produced doll clothes.

The Humpty Dumpty Doll Hospital was the same hospital referenced in the first letter that was intercepted by the censors and then given to the FBI. Mrs. Clear was the creator of the first American made china doll as well as many other china, Parian and blonde bisque dolls. Renowned for her high quality, finely made reproduction china heads, she also produced some all-original, non-reproduction dolls, including portraits of George and Martha Washington made in the same manner as antique dolls.

Fortunately for the investigating FBI agents, Mr. and Mrs. Clear had complete correspondence files of other doll collectors from around the world in which they had saved, among other things, post cards written by Velvalee to Mrs. Clear from almost every city she had visited. These handwritten notes served as a comprehensive itinerary, revealing the routes through various states in which the Dickinsons had traveled, as well as the dates and the hotels where they stayed.

FBI laboratory forensic examination of all five letters confirmed that the signatures on the letters were forgeries but had been copied from original signatures in the possession of the forger. The examination also showed that the typewriter used in the preparation of the letters was different in each case, but the typing characteristics indicated that the letters were prepared by the same person.

All five letters used code text or open code, referred to by the FBI agents in this particular case as "doll code." This was itself encoded, and the stegotext, or steganography—the deliberate concealment of data within other data—was the doll orders which related information concerning the repair of dolls, the mounting of dolls, and the dressing of dolls. The dolls were described with reference to their nationality and activities and as to the extent of the repairs necessary and where these repairs were being performed. It was this information which described vital information about U.S. Armed Forces, their ability to defend the United States, and particularly the ships of the U.S. Navy, their location, condition, and repair, with special emphasis on the damage of such vessels at Pearl Harbor.

Except for the first letter that had been intercepted by the censors, the last four letters had been returned to the address of origination that was typed on the envelopes with the "recipient unknown" notation. All five letters were addressed to the same individual in Buenos Aires, a Señora Ines Lopez de Molinali at 2563 O'Higgins Street.

In each case, the persons whose names had appeared on the envelopes as the senders stated that the signatures on the letters resembled theirs and that the letters contained some correct information about their personal lives and interest in dolls. All emphatically denied, however, that they had sent any of the letters.

There was one other significant common element that each of the five letters shared, and that was a connection to the owner of an exclusive doll shop in uptown New York with the prestigious Madison Avenue address.

ꕤ

Chapter 4

The Investigation

During their investigation into the letters, the FBI had been informed by the woman from Oregon that she had offered Valvalee Dickinson and her husband a place to stay in her home whenever they traveled to Oregon now that her daughter was married and no longer living with her parents. She explained that Velvalee was an antique doll dealer, lecturer, and collector well respected in all doll circles of that day. In fact, even though the woman hadn't purchased a doll in quite some time, Velvalee continued to send her dolls on approval, usually once a month. Without even realizing it, she and Velvalee had developed a long-standing correspondence between them in which she had shared personal information.

Interestingly, the woman from Colorado Springs also provided information that directed the FBI's attention to Velvalee Dickinson, the doll shop owner located in New York City with whom she too had done business. She was concerned that Mrs. Dickinson had used her signature on one of the letters in a spirit of vindictiveness because the woman had purchased some dolls from Mrs. Dickinson and had been unable to pay for them promptly. Another woman then came forward claiming that she also felt her signature had been used out of spite by the seemingly shy and noncommittal woman who owned the exclusive doll shop in New York.

It soon became apparent that the one connection between all of the women who had received the returned letters had at some point corresponded with Velvalee Dickinson, thereby providing Velvalee with their hand-written signatures. Based on their conclusions, the FBI initiated a formal espionage investigation into whether Velvalee Dickinson was passing military information to the enemy in this manner.

Lee Dickinson died on March 30, 1943, and on April 1, 1943, a service was held for Velvalee's late husband at the James McLarney Funeral Parlor in New York City. Afterwards, the body was then taken in a zinc-lined casket to Woodlawn Cemetery, Bronx, New York, where it was retained. A short time later, Velvalee took her husband's body to California to be interred at the Cypress Lawn Cemetery just outside of San Francisco. From there, at the suggestion of a bank official, Mr. C.L. Lesourd, she went to Seattle, Washington, to file her late husband's will and settle his estate. According to Velvalee, this was what her late husband had requested even though he was born in Philadelphia.

When Velvalee returned to New York after settling her late husband's estate, she got an apartment with her brother in the same building where her doll shop was located. She remarked to a neighbor at the time that she wished the war was over because it interfered with her being able to import foreign costume dolls.

Velvalee struggled to maintain her lifestyle on Madison Avenue until suddenly her financial situation suspiciously changed. On several occasions she was seen holding a fist full of one-hundred-dollar bills, something unheard of during this time of war. She used the bills to pay her doll shop employee's salary as well as other debts she had incurred in personal loans. Some of Velvalee's more extravagant purchases included audio recordings of Japanese music, which a maid complained she frequently had to return.

Francis M. Dickinson, Velvalee's brother-in-law, became suspicious, and on behalf of his family reported to Assistant United States Attorney Edward C. Wallace and the interviewing FBI agent on May 19, 1944, that taking the body to California was against the expressed wishes of his brother. It was his opinion that Velvalee had secreted money or other material of value in Lee's casket at the James McLarney Funeral Parlor in New York City prior to the removal of the remains first to the church and then to the Woodlawn Cemetery.

According to Francis Dickinson, Velvalee had insisted that she be left alone with the open casket where she remained for approximately 45 minutes following the service. Lee Dickinson's relatives, the funeral director, as well as the cemetery employees regarded Velvalee's activities suspicious at the time. As a result of the interview, the San Francisco Field Division contacted the United States Attorney in that judicial district to ascertain the legal process necessary to open Lee Dickinson's casket, but it led to no further investigation.

At the same time, Mrs. George Ernhart, Lee Dickinson's mother, revealed in an FBI interview that her son had died penniless. In spite of this, it was later determined through the FBI's investigation that a check dated July 3, 1942, in the amount of $2,000 payable to Lee Taylor Dickinson, was drawn on the Seattle First National Bank with the notation "Lee T. Dickinson for deposit Velvalee M. Dickinson." It was noted that this payment was made by a trust check drawn on the Seattle First National Bank, Seattle, Washington, as probated on the estate of Lee Taylor Dickinson, King County, Seattle, Washington, Clerk's file #85295. C.L. Lesourd of Seattle First National Bank, would later testify under subpoena that "Mrs. Dickinson advised him on March 30, 1943, that she was very anxious to receive as much money as possible from the Ella and John Godwin estate because at the time of her husband's death on March 29, 1943, he had left her absolutely nothing other than the one-fifth interest in said estate."

Over a period of several months, FBI agents visited the exclusive, up-town doll shop on Madison Avenue pretending to be customers, all the while observing, listening, and examining the situation. The owner, Velvalee Dickinson, was a small, elegant, and charming widow, according to the agents. Usually plainly dressed in brown or sometimes blue, she was described as attractive, being less than 5 feet tall, weighing no more than 100 pounds, with a small lively face.

Neighbors were less kind in their portrayal of Velvalee, describing her as mousy, drab, and dull with a shrill, strident voice. She wore plain brown skirts and jackets primarily, they noticed, and her facial features and quick movements appeared more bird-like than attractive.

In her business dealings, she was a fast and excited talker, clear and convincing, and not easily confused, the agents noticed. On many occasions they observed that she was cantankerous to customers who came in just to browse, and she came across as arrogant on the telephone to the secretaries or assistants who were calling on behalf of her well-heeled clients. On the other hand, she was pleasant to her wealthy customers, especially if there appeared to be a sale in the making. And although she wore glasses, she didn't show her fifty years.

A luxury store for both amateurs and educated collectors, the Velvalee Dickinson doll shop, the FBI discovered, was well known not only in New York, but throughout the United States, and included among its clientele many well-known and recognized names. The sign above the entrance was painted in blue letters:

VELVALEE DICKINSON

ANCIENT DOLLS – FOREIGN – REGIONALS

Much of the merchandise was rare and, except for those special dolls Velvalee advertised for her less affluent customers, did not include dolls under twenty-five dollars. Antique dolls from the Colonial period were priced at five hundred dollars and more. Also priced at three figures or more, there were porcelain dolls dating back to Victor Hugo's Paris; exquisite figurines from the time of Marie Antoinette; dolls from pioneer times; bizarre idols carved in wood by the indigenous people of Dutch Guinness; and round-faced dolls dressed in delicate silk brocade that represented China.

The shop itself looked like something between a museum and a puppet theater. The large, valance-draped window looking out onto Madison Avenue was decorated tastefully, and groups of dolls in different poses were entertainingly arranged on a small platform or stage with scenery.

At the same time they were surveilling Velvalee's doll shop activities, the FBI agents were also investigating her background both in New York and California. Using her maiden name Bluehar and variations of the spelling, such as Blucher, Bleicher and Bliicher, they determined that her lineage traced back to the Prussian general Bliicher who had fought against Napoleon.

In addition, they learned that Lee Dickinson, her husband, while living in California, had his San Francisco office in the same building that housed the German and Japanese Consulates. Velvalee's work references at both the bank and the agriculture commodity brokerage company in San Francisco were excellent. She and her husband had lived in the Imperial quarter known as El Centro in the Imperial Valley where Lee conducted most of his business. This was in the heart of the Japanese colony where many of the Japanese farmers had settled.

With Velvalee's strong innate business skills and almost obsessive interest in the Japanese culture, the FBI agents discovered, she served for many years as a commercial mediator between the Japanese and the Americans. Velvalee had no criminal record, but her name was among the members of the American-Japanese

Society until 1937 when she moved from California to New York.

Once in New York, she worked for a time in the Bloomingdale's doll department where she made a considerable number of sales, and then eventually established her own doll shop on Madison Avenue. Her business relationships included clients in all forty-eight states, and she often made business trips, especially to the West Coast, to visit some of her famous Hollywood clients.

The FBI's investigation revealed that in the early and mid-1930s, while she was still in the San Francisco area, Velvalee had been a member of the Japanese American Society, her dues paid for a time by an attaché of the Japanese Consulate in San Francisco. It was also determined that she had made frequent visits to the Japanese Consulate in that city, attended important social functions in which Japanese Navy members and other high-ranking government officials were present, and she had invited many Japanese friends and acquaintances to soirées in her home for the purpose of entertaining them. On several of these occasions, she wore the "wafuku," authentic Japanese attire that included beautifully embroidered silk kimonos, the "hanao" footwear with "tabi" socks and "geta," and decorative headwear.

In addition, the FBI learned that after moving to New York City, Velvalee had visited the Nippon Club and the Japan Institute, had cultivated the friendship of the Japanese Consul General there, and had met Ichiro Yokoyama, the Japanese Naval Attaché from Washington, DC.

When the FBI traced Velvalee's activities from January 1942 through June 1942, the time frame in which the five doll letters had been sent, the FBI found that Velvalee and her husband had been in the areas from which the letters had been postmarked and at the time the letters were sent. Hotels in San Francisco, Los Angeles, and Chicago where the couple had stayed were also located, and the FBI examination showed that typewriters made available for guests to rent at these hotels were used in writing the four letters sent to Argentina.

Further FBI investigation into the Dickinson's finances disclosed that Velvalee had consistently borrowed money from banks and business associates, as well as friends, in New York City as late as 1941. During the last years of her husband's life, Velvalee found herself in debt and was struggling financially because of the expenses brought on by Lee Dickinson's medical condition. He suffered from a chronic heart disease, a complication of Bright's disease, which because of its severity necessitated full-time medical assistance at home, regular visits from his doctor—Dr. Conroy, and expensive stays in the clinic.

However, that changed in 1943 when she suddenly began to make expensive cash purchases. It was also at that time when she was observed on several occasions to have had in her possession a large number of $100 bills. Four of the bills which she had used in transactions were traced by the FBI to Japanese official sources who had received the money before the war.

Another incident that would get reported by the *Boston Globe* at a later date occurred when federal agents showed up at the New York apartment where 13-year-old Lee Lawrence Pierce and her mother lived to take away Perla, a Mexican gypsy rag doll belonging to the young teen. When it was returned to the young girl a few weeks later, "there was a coarse, zigzagging stitch across its smooth cotton, neck, evidence of a crude decapitation," Lee Pierce recalls. She would learn years later that the FBI suspected Velvalee of hiding coded messages inside the heads of dolls but never found any proof.

Lee Pierce had acquired the doll only a few days earlier from Young's Bookstore located next to Velvalee's doll shop on Madison Avenue. The young teenager had begged Jo Kimball, the owner of the bookstore, to let her hold it when a woman wearing red high-heeled shoes, as she remembered, suddenly appeared from behind a curtain and angrily snatched the doll away.

It was a few days later that the determined Lee Pierce returned to the book store with a small bag of coins, this time with the intention of paying for the doll with her year's allowance of saved quarters and dimes totaling ten dollars. This time she was in luck, for on that day the book store owner let her take the doll, explaining that its owner had left it behind.

As happy as Lee Pierce was to take the doll, it would be the angry woman wearing red high-heeled shoes rebuking her, she should have known better than to handle a doll that wasn't hers, that would stay vivid in her memory.

The FBI gathered information and observed Velvalee Dickinson for weeks without taking any definitive position or action until suddenly their suspicions were confirmed. Hidden inside the tissue packaging of several boxes with dolls destined to distant collectors that had been confiscated by the U.S. Postal Service were found short tickets describing the dolls written in a kind of childish language.

This could have been something used within the doll collecting trade itself, but the agents surmised it could also be a code. One in particular was a penny wooden doll that had a tiny purse on the front of her dress. Inside the purse was a coded message concerning treasonable information given to her by Japanese Allies.

Meanwhile, Velvalee was growing anxious and uncomfortable. Without her husband around to take care of the financial end of her business, she complained to a neighbor that she was now all alone in the world other than her brother, and that she missed her husband, both at home and in her business.

Her shop seemed to be drawing suspicious clients whose questions indicated they obviously knew nothing about antique dolls or any other kind of dolls. There were more men that came into her shop now, just looking around and lingering, but not buying anything. And for months, she hadn't received any orders or instructions from her Japanese contact.

Yet she had been so careful and meticulous in her planning, she tried to reassure herself. Surely, if she were suspected of any wrongdoing, at the very least she would have been questioned.

Even so, the doubt and uncertainty started to build as she tried to reason through the situation. For example, there was a New England doll merchant who had been angry with her for taking away several of his Hollywood clients. Believing her to be untrustworthy, he had even accused her of falsifying some of the old dolls, adulterating the costumes.

The truth was, Velvalee had falsified dolls, but the collectors she dealt with would never have noticed. And she had sold the dolls—both authentic and false—at good prices. When this particular collector delivered his own collection to Velvalee to be sold, he took a policeman with him to make sure he was paid in full.

More and more she was having difficulty sleeping, and, therefore, decided that a trip to the West Coast was in order. She would try to meet with a former Japanese navy officer who she knew was hiding in Portland, Oregon. If anything had happened, he would have escaped to Mexico and from there have gotten picked up by a Japanese submarine and taken to safety.

Florence B. Hoblin had worked for Velvalee at the doll store a short time in the early 1940s before becoming the personal secretary to General Joseph McNarney and relocating to Germany. While still working for him, in November 1945, General McNarney became commanding general of the U.S. Forces in the European Theater and commander in chief, U.S. Forces of Occupation in Germany. When Florence returned to the United States in 1947, she married H. Sherwood Flather, who worked with the Bureau of National Affairs in Washington, DC.

Velvalee had replaced Florence with Alma, a trusted, efficient employee who could handle the shop and even negotiate doll prices when necessary. Also, unlike Florence, she didn't have any ties with the U.S. Government. She would let her know if anything happened in her absence. If the FBI did search the shop,

Velvalee wouldn't be there and she would have time to escape out of the country.

But all of these thoughts were the distraught musings of an active imagination brought on by sleepless nights. Early one morning after a particularly difficult, sleepless night, she went to the shop and instructed Alma to go to the bank and withdraw some money in order that she could leave the store with adequate funds on hand. She was going to Florida and perhaps Canada, she told Alma, giving her false destinations in order to conceal her true plan. She also told Alma that her brother, Oswald, would visit the store from time to time in case anything needed to be done.

Velvalee then took a taxi to Saks on 34th Street, all the while glancing back, fearful she was being followed. At Saks, she crossed the overhead bridge which led to Gimbel's Department Store and hurriedly descended into the maze of basement underpasses that connected to Gimbel's and the underground subway. Terrified she was being followed, without even stopping to purchase a ticket, she went through the gate and boarded the next outgoing train which happened to be bound for Philadelphia. She paid her fare to the conductor and decided to continue on to Chicago, and from there on to Portland, Oregon.

When she finally arrived in Portland, she immediately went to the Chinese restaurant where her contact worked, but to her horror, displayed in the window between two cactus plants was a sign: "Closed." Panic once again filled her thoughts.

The possibility of getting in touch with other contacts in California was tenuous at best since most of her Japanese friends and associates had been either moved or interred to one of the camps on the West Coast. This was the result of President Roosevelt's Executive Order 9066 which he signed on February 19, 1942, authorizing the Secretary of War to prescribe certain areas as military zones and the removal of any or all people from these zones "as deemed necessary or desirable."

With the intention of preventing espionage within the United States, the military in turn defined the entire West Coast, home to the majority of Americans of Japanese ancestry or citizenship, as a military area. By June, more than 110,000 Japanese Americans were relocated to remote internment camps built by the U.S. military in scattered locations around the country where they would remain for the next two and a half years. Trying to locate anyone at these camps would be extremely difficult, not to mention draw unwanted attention.

Velvalee stayed in California for a few weeks, going through the motions as if nothing was wrong, uncertain of what to do, and trying to convince herself that had the FBI discovered what she had been doing, they would have arrested her a long time ago. Once again, she relied on Harry Jeffs, the real estate agent who handled her late husband's property, to drive her around the San Francisco area and taking time to order hand-made Indian dolls. She even considered closing her store in New York and moving back to the West Coast.

With that in mind, she offered $15,000 as part interest in a hotel. This amount was approximately twice what she had received from the life insurance left by her late husband. When that didn't work out and she eventually did return to New York, it was with the discouraging, uncomfortable realization that she had accomplished nothing, and her feelings of anxiety were stronger than ever.

Velvalee continued to conduct herself as she normally would, and when the Christmas season approached, she agreed to let Bloomingdale's promotion department use several dozen of her dolls in an attractive window display when they asked her about it.

Through the holidays and into the new year, the FBI were examining every detail of Velvalee's life and even went about trying to identify the origin of the paper on which the letters were written. They observed that her most recent letters had a tone of desperation as she asked for "money" and "answers."

By prolonging any arrest action, they hoped to be able to identify and catch her accomplices. It would also give them time to warn their South American offices of the true contents of Velvalee's doll boxes and perhaps gather more information about the people she was dealing with. Now, however, with the insurmountable evidence they had against Velvalee Dickinson, and the fact that their investigation was approaching a year in which they had been working the "Doll Woman" case, they were ready to take their next step.

ꕥ ❋ ꕥ

Velvalee Dickinson

Alderson, West Virginia, Correctional Institution of Women

Mildred Elizabeth Gillars a.k.a. "Axis Sally"

TODAY'S WEATHER

The Herald

CITY EDITION

NIPPON PLANES BOMB AND SINK U.S. GUNBOAT PANAY

ALL SET FOR TOMORROW'S P.I. ELECTIONS

JAPANESE STOP U. S. DESTROYER AIDING HOOVER

EVACUEES FROM NANKING ABOARD SHIP WHEN HIT

NEW MERALCO RATES OKAYED

NATIONALISTS ARE EXPECTED TO WIN MANILA

FIND CASHIER SHORT P5,000

MOROS REOCCUPY CAPTURED COTTA

MANILA RESIDENT GRANTED DIVORCE

NANKING'S FALL EXPECTED SOON

Bombing of U.S. Gunboat *Panay*

Doll Used in Transmitting Coded Messages

Early English Wax over Wood Dolls in Velvalee's Collection

Elizebeth Friedman

Eunice Kennedy Shriver

Former Velvalee Dickinson's Doll Store
718 Madison Ave, New York, NT

Historic Old Cemetery - Sacramento

J. Edgar Hoover

Lilly Barbara Carola Stein – "Duquesne" Spy

Mare Island, Naval Shipyard in 1946

Mare Island, Shipyard Drydock

O'Higgins Street, Buenos Aires, Argentina

Perla Negra

President Franklin D. Roosevelt

Secretary of State Cordell Hull

Spanish Gypsy Doll in Velvalee's Collection

Special Agent in Charge Robert L. Shivers

The Attack on Pearl Harbor

The Store Front of Velvalee Dickinson's Doll Store
718 Madison Ave., New York, NY

Iva Toguri D'Aquino a.k.a. "Tokyo Rose"

USS *Louisville* (CA-28) - 1945

USS *Louisville* (CA-28), at Mare Island during refitting, new guns, new radar and fire controller - Aug - Dec 1942

USS *Louisville* (CA-28) - 1945

USS *Panay* (PR-5)

USS *Saratoga* (CV-3), Aircraft on the flight deck, preparing for launching, circa 1929-30

USS *Saratoga* (CV-3), Launching planes, circa summer 1941

USS *Shaw* (DD-373), Exploding - Pearl Harbor 7 Dec 41

USS *Shaw* (DD-373), Pearl Harbor 7 Dec 41
After Explosion of the Forward Magazine

USS *Shaw* (DD-373), With Temporary Bow

USS *Shaw* (DD-373) - 1942 With New Bow

Velvalee Dickinson

Chapter 5

The Arrest and Indictment

On January 21, 1944, federal agents followed Velvalee Dickinson to a bank in Midtown Manhattan and into a vault where she had unlocked her safety deposit box and was going through its contents. They immediately arrested her. A short time later, her arrest was announced by FBI Special Agent E.E. Conroy.

Velvalee Dickinson "fought bitterly, kicking, clawing, and screaming in an attempt to escape," he commented, something that was immediately picked up and described with as much titillating detail as possible in numerous newspapers across the country. "Mrs.

Dickinson sent many coded messages to South America containing military and naval information vital to our security and valuable to our enemies," said Special Agent Conroy. The coded messages were "concealed in what appeared to be innocent letters discussing sales of dolls.... She signed the letters with forged names of her customers," he explained, but citing national security, he refused to reveal the contents of the coded messages.

In an appearance before U.S. Commissioner Garret W. Cotter late in the day, Velvalee was accompanied by her brother, Oswald Blucher, who was still living with her at the time and assisted in running the shop whenever she was away. Federal attorneys asked that the bail be set for $35,000; however, bail was finally set at $25,000 after representatives of Velvalee's attorney, Arthur Garfield Hays, vigorously protested a higher amount. Even so, a $25,000 bail at that time was certainly a large amount, indicating the seriousness of the charges and suggesting that the government considered Velvalee dangerous. "I'll write a check," snapped Velvalee, still defiant, "if they'll return my checkbooks."

Examination of the contents of the safe deposit box disclosed some $15,940 in cash, of which $10,000 was in $100 Federal Reserve Notes. Many of the Notes were traced to the Yokohama Specie Bank in New York. A portion of the money had been in the hands of Captain Yuzo Ishikawa of the Japanese Naval Inspector's Office in New York City before coming into the possession of Velvalee.

It would be reported before the trial that additional money and values were confiscated and estimated to be valued in the amount of $40,000, roughly equivalent to what she owed to the authorities for unpaid taxes. The Internal Revenue Service immediately put a lien on the funds.

All total, it was calculated that Velvalee received approximately $60,000 for her work as a spy for the Imperial Japanese Government. This would later be estimated as the highest amount paid by the Japanese to a spy during World War II.

After flinging the metal box and its contents at the arresting agents before being physically carried from the bank, Velvalee told them at the time that the money in the safe deposit box had come from insurance companies, a savings account, and her doll business. When asked why she hadn't placed some of her funds in U.S. War Bonds, she responded by saying she didn't know how to buy them.

During a subsequent interview, however, Velvalee explained that the money in the box had actually come from her husband; that she had "found a big wad of cash and the code under the mattress cover of her husband's bed immediately after his death." She stated that her husband had not told her the source of the money, but she believed it might have come from the Japanese Consul in New York City.

Refusing to be fingerprinted, she once again put up a struggle, rebelling until being convinced by the judge that if she didn't cooperate, she would be forced. As Velvalee was escorted away, she covered her face in front of photographers, all the while attempting to proclaim in a high-pitched voice her innocence and minimize the seriousness of the charges against her.

Three weeks later, on February 11, 1944, she was indicted by the federal grand jury in the Southern District of New York on a charge of having tried to circumvent the censorship regulations by sending letters to Argentina that contained coded messages concerning vital defense information. The names or types of dolls were said to have formed the basis of the alleged code, argued Edward C. Wallace, assistant United States attorney and unrelated to Mary Wallace, one of the victims of Velvalee's coded letter-writing. He characterized the letters as dangerous when arraigning her before Federal Judge Vincent L. Leibell, and asked that her bail be continued at $25,000, the figure set following her arrest on January 21. The court agreed and adjourned the case to February 21, one month later.

At the same time, Judge Leibell also ruled that Velvalee's brother, Oswald (Ossie) Blucher, could not visit his sister while she awaited trial at the Women's House of Detention, 10 Greenwich Avenue, New York City. The ban was ordered after Assistant U.S. Attorney Edward C. Wallace informed the court on how Blucher tried to slip a little black notebook to his sister during an interview on January 24, three days after her arrest. Even though the notebook was described as being black, it was probably Velvalee's small blue address book that contained the names of several Japanese high-ranking officials and others. This was held in evidence as Exhibit 44.

Suspected of containing the Japanese codes that Velvalee used, Wallace explained how FBI Special Agent

Gerald Driscoll, who was sitting nearby during the interview, thwarted four attempts by Blucher to give the notebook to his sister. In addition, Velvalee attempted to pass several notes to her brother during that same interview, all of which were prevented by the agent present. The following day, at the request of Velvalee's attorney, Maurice Shaine, because Oswald appeared to be mentally and physically ill, Judge Leibell reversed his decision and agreed to let Oswald Blucher visit his sister, but only when FBI agents were present.

Violation of the censorship statute and a conviction could result in a maximum penalty of ten years in prison and a $10,000 fine. Espionage, on the other hand, if proven, could result in the death penalty. Velvalee faced prosecution by U.S. Attorney James B.M. McNally, who had a 98 percent conviction rate which included, among others, the conviction and stripping of citizenship from Erika Segnitz Field, a New York woman who'd trained her parrot to scream "Heil Hitler!"

Velvalee pleaded not guilty during her arraignment and, unable to raise the money, was held in lieu of the $25,000 bail. "Who are all of these people?" Velvalee asked as she was being led away, apparently not aware that her case had stirred so much national interest. In order to fulfill the requirements of the New York Bertillon files, a photograph of the defendant—or "mug shot," was required. However, Velvalee once again resisted and yelled, "No photographs!" Commissioner Cotter temporarily honored that request but refused another: Velvalee could not take her Japanese music recordings or her record player with her to jail.

Two attorneys were appointed by Judge Grover M. Moscowitz on February 28, 1944, to defend Velvalee, whose trial was scheduled on the federal court calendar for April 3. Even though Velvalee had substantial funds at the time of her arrest, they were now tied up by income tax liens on the federal taxes she owed, and as evidence in the case against her. She had no other known source of income. Therefore, declining to choose any of a group of lawyers suggested by Velvalee, Judge Moscowitz named Aaron Samuelson, 260 East 161st Street, the Bronx, and Maurice L. Shaine, 295 Madison Avenue to defend her.

The U.S. Government's evidence included the Federal Reserve Notes found in the bank safety deposit box and the testimony of confidential informants. In addition, there was the forensic proof concerning the Argentina-bound letters. The signatures on the letters were forged and each letter had been prepared using different hotel typewriters rented by the Dickinsons. Furthermore, the dates and locations of their postings coincided with the Dickinsons' travels to areas where the letters supposedly originated, information that was corroborated by the extensive correspondence files of Mama and Papa Clear.

In their search for evidence, the FBI had found a portable typewriter in Velvalee's Madison Avenue doll shop, and forensic experts determined that it had been used to type the letter supposedly written by Mary Wallace of Springfield, Ohio. According to the government, the treasonous activity fell apart when the FBI discovered that Señora Ines Lopez de Molinali, 2563 O'Higgins Street, Buenos Aires, Argentina, was, in fact, a Japanese spy, and the Imperial Japanese Government, unknown to Velvalee, had deactivated the address in Buenos Aires used to retrieve espionage reports, causing her letters to be returned.

FBI cryptographers were prepared to testify to the messages contained in the letters themselves. They alleged that Velvalee used a rudimentary form of "open code," of which there are three types: the jargon code, the null cipher, and the geometrical systems. However, the cryptographers determined that it was the jargon code that Velvalee specifically used, where an apparently innocuous word stood for the real term in a text contrived to seem as bland and as innocent as possible. In this case, it was dolls.

One of the oldest codes known in cryptology, jargon codes can range from the most informal sort of code to a full code list. In Velvalee's five letters, she substituted entire words instead of individual letters to pass secrets to the Japanese Imperial Government on American warship conditions and locations. Applying the jargon code, the three "dolls" mentioned in Mrs. Wallace's letter were three U.S. Navy ships under repair in West Coast shipyards. The "old fisherman with a net over his back" was an aircraft carrier shielded by an anti-submarine net; the "old woman with wood on her back" was a wooden-decked battleship; and the "little boy" was a destroyer.

Even with numerous typographical and grammatical errors, and all written in a sort of familiar, disconnected feminine style sprinkled with personal references, alert FBI cryptanalysts easily ascertained the true meaning of the coded letters.

A few weeks after Velvalee's arrest, her 40-year-old brother, Oswald Blucher, received a ten-day jail sentence from Federal Judge Simon H. Rifkind. The court's action was announced on March 31, 1944, by United States Attorney James B.M. McNally who had cited Blucher for "contumacious conduct" when under subpoena to testify before a federal grand jury.

"The nature of Blucher's offense was not disclosed, and the investigation concerned was not identified," reported the April 1, 1944, issue of the *New York Times.* "Edward C. Wallace, assistant United States attorney said, however, that his inquiry on Blucher's sister, Mrs. Velvalee Dickinson, dealer in rare dolls, was continuing."

Even though Oswald was jailed on a somewhat veiled and ambiguous charge, his ten-day jail sentence was handed down just a little over eight weeks from the time Velvalee had been arrested in the bank vault. And, she had already been indicted by the federal grand jury in the Southern District of New York for violation of the censorship statutes, conviction of which could result in a maximum penalty of ten years in prison and a $10,000 fine.

He had been warned once soon after her arrest when he tried to pass the little black book, possibly containing Japanese codes, to Velvalee and accept written messages from her while she was waiting for her trial in the Women's House of Detention. It is more than likely that he was expected to testify for the prosecution in Velvalee's trial, but rather than being cooperative, Oswald chose to be loyal to his sister. He insisted that Velvalee knew she was being investigated by the FBI and, therefore, the fact that she didn't try to leave the country meant that she was innocent.

The court didn't agree.

In examining correspondence and telephone messages between Velvalee and her brother, it was learned that Velvalee was opposed to any agreement with the government and that she would "delay and delay and wait" until she could obtain money from the Treasury Department, then break with her court-appointed attorneys Samuclson and Shainc and rctain Ncw York attorncy James D.C. Murray who specialized in criminal defense.

Oswald not only agreed with Velvalee, he counselled her. In addition, he indicated that he had removed all of the contents of the doll store at 718 Madison Avenue to their apartment and was in the process of disposing of the merchandise.

Meanwhile, the FBI continued to build their case against the "Doll Woman." Shortly after the agents arrested Velvalee, Edward C. Wallace, assistant United States attorney, called the supervisor of the FBI's New York office to ask if the Bureau had any objection if the federal prosecution showed the letters to cryptographer expert Elizebeth Smith Friedman. Friedman, noted as "America's first female cryptanalyst," had made a significant name for herself in code-breaking against international smuggling and drug running in various parts of the world as well as wartime enemies.

In addition to her cryptanalytic successes, she was frequently called to testify in cases against accused parties. She had also played a major role in settling a dispute between Canadian and U.S. governments over the true ownership of a sailing vessel called the *I'm Alone*, suspected of smuggling liquor into the United States. It was flying the Canadian flag when it was sunk by a U.S. Coast Guard cutter for failing to heed a "heave to and be searched" signal. The Canadian government filed a $350,000 suit against the U.S., but the intelligence information uncovered from the twenty-three messages decoded by Mrs. Friedman indicated *de facto* U.S. ownership just as the U.S. government had originally suspected. As a consequence, the law suit was dropped, and the owner of the ship—a U.S. citizen—was identified and captured.

Assistant U.S. Attorney Wallace had worked with Friedman in the past and hoped to get her opinion on the "Doll Woman's" letters; specifically, the code used. Even though FBI cryptographers had thoroughly examined the five letters and supported the theory that Velvalee had used a secret "doll code" thus violating U.S. censorship laws, the prosecution felt it wouldn't hurt to have the professional and unbiased opinion of an international expert in cryptography.

Wallace's request provoked an exchange of at least eight phone calls, teletype messages, and memos that traveled up the chain of command from the FBI's New York office to Washington, and ultimately to the desk of FBI Director J. Edgar Hoover. The gist of these communications was that the prosecutor wanted Elizebeth's expertise and spoke highly of her. "Mrs. Friedman and her husband, who is a cryptographer for the Army, are recognized as the leading authorities in the country and have written numerous books on the subject," the attorney wrote. However, the FBI agents, and notably Director Hoover—always seeking ways to enhance the

Agency's image—worried that Elizebeth would siphon publicity from the bureau and steal its spotlight. In fact, C.A. Appel of the FBI Technical Laboratory had been working with the case from the beginning analyzing the letters and had been the first to interpret the code.

The New York office sent Hoover a teletype on March 18, 1944: "Advise as to submission questioned letters to Elizebeth Friedman for examination." Hoover responded: "Concerning the project to submit the documents to Mrs. Friedman… There appears no point is to be gained by multiplying the number of examiners." Since he posed no formal objection, however, Assistant U.S. Attorney Wallace went ahead and sent Elizebeth the "Doll Woman's" letters.

Elizebeth analyzed Velvalee's correspondence and sent the prosecutor a five-page letter before traveling to New York at the feds' expense to discuss the case with him in person.

> *My dear Mr. Wallace,*
>
> *Within the last two days I have spent a few hours examining the Dickinson letters. I am setting forth here some queries and statements which may be accepted for what they are worth, mindful of your statement on the telephone that you hope*

> *to obtain 'leads,' and that you understand that the code in the letters is the 'intangible' type of method not susceptible to scientific proof.*

After making it clear that this was not the usual sort of cryptanalysis that she did, that this was only her opinion, Elizebeth went on to discuss what she thought the "Doll Woman" was really talking about when she talked about dolls.

Confirming what the FBI cryptologists had already determined, the letters, she said, were a textbook example of "open code," a way of communicating secretly out in the open without necessarily arousing suspicion. "Granddaughter's doll" in one letter might refer to a U.S. ship that had been damaged at Pearl Harbor and was being repaired. "Family" meant the Japanese fleet. "English dolls" meant three classes of English ships, such as a battleship, battlecruiser, or destroyer. Where Dickinson wrote, "One of these three dolls is an old Fisherman with a Net over his back" and "another is an old woman with wood on her back" and the third is "a little boy," she probably meant, "One of these three warships is a minesweeper, and another is a warship with superstructure, and the third is a small warship.

(Destroyer? Torpedo boat? Auxiliary warship?)" Elizebeth guessed.

Elizebeth also pointed out that the street number of the address in the five letters to Señora Ines Lopez de Molinali in Buenos Aires was given as five different numbers that included 1414 O'Higgins and 2563 O'Higgins, suggesting a new theory not yet considered by the FBI that the messages were never meant to even reach their destination; and were intended instead to be intercepted en route, in an airline pouch or a censorship office, by a friendly Axis confederate.

Elizebeth's letter showed her analytical brilliance; it also showed her native cautiousness in that she was reluctant to say anything that couldn't absolutely be proven. Words in an open code can have multiple meanings, and she didn't want to testify in court for this reason.

Another reason for preferring not to testify in court was, given the fact that she was a woman working in a highly technical and specialized field usually reserved only for men, she was hounded unmercifully by the press about things that had nothing to do with whatever case she was working on ("Do you like to bake?" "What is your favorite color?"). A poet and Shakespeare scholar who preferred her privacy, Elizebeth didn't want to discuss her personal life—whether she liked to bake or not, or her color preference—nor did she appreciate being put in the spotlight.

Hoover saw the open code differently. To him, the vagueness of an open code was an advantage, not a disadvantage, enabling his agents "to give the more extended estimates and alternative possibilities" during cross-examination.

Meanwhile, information compiled as a result of the FBI's continuing investigation resulted in another indictment of Velvalee on May 5, 1944, this time on charges of violating the espionage statutes, the censorship statutes, and the Registration Act of 1917 which was intended "to prohibit interference with military operations or recruitment, to prevent insubordination in the military, and to prevent the support of United States enemies during wartime." In 1919, the Supreme Court of the United States had ruled unanimously through *Schenk v. United States* that the act did not violate the freedom of speech of those convicted under its provisions.

"This woman reported the movements and repairs of battleships after Pearl Harbor to the enemy," United States Attorney James B.M. McNally told Federal Judge William Bondy, to whom the indictment was handed up. Though the FBI 's first firm evidence of Velvalee's espionage was the returned letter she sent to Buenos Aires in February 1942, she was suspected of relaying information on U.S. destroyers before Japan's December 7, 1941, attack on Pearl Harbor. The surprise bombing raid killed or wounded more than thirty-five hundred Americans and decimated the U.S. Pacific Fleet in less than two hours. "We charge that she did this for money received from Japanese agents," McNally further contended.

The charge of espionage was an offense that carried the death penalty in wartime, or a prison term up to thirty years. "So far," wrote the *Washington Sunday Star*, "on this side of the water, Mrs. Dickinson is the woman spy of this war."

The *New York Times* reported Velvalee's appearance at the federal court as "drab." Looking more subdued than previous appearances in court, she wore a black hat with imitation white flowers fastened on it.

Velvalee pleaded not guilty, and her bail of $25,000 was continued.

With this new indictment, Judge William Bondy set her trial down for June 5, moved from the earlier trial date of April 3, with the understanding that the government would not oppose a further postponement if her assigned counsel had not prepared her defense by that time.

The question of the trial date once again came up when counsel of the defense, Aaron Samuelson, requested a two-month adjournment until July 10. In addition, at the same time Velvalee's other defense lawyer, Maurice L. Shaine, disclosed that he was seeking release of $25,000 of the defendant's funds tied up by an income tax lien filed by the Bureau of Internal Revenue. "A substantial part of it has been described by Mr. Wallace as evidence in the government's case against Mrs. Dickinson," the *New York Times* reported on June 6, 1944.

As her trial date neared, it became increasingly obvious that Velvalee had been living far beyond her means. Internal Revenue files revealed that Velvalee Dickinson's total income reported in 1939 was $2,616.20. In 1942, she claimed a loss in the amount of $1,135.67.

Federal Tax Collector for the Third District, James W. Johnson, set the amount owed by Velvalee in the amount of $40,132. This included back taxes for the years 1940, 1941, and 1942, and the amount the Internal Revenue Service had calculated that she owed for the year 1943. In addition, there were penalties and fines totaling $2,001.

On July 10, 1944, in federal court, Judge Stephen Brennan granted another delay, but only until July 31 after United States Attorney James B.M. McNally vehemently opposed a longer, sixty-day adjournment requested by defense counsel.

Velvalee had been in jail, unable to raise the required bail of $25,000, since her arrest in January. Her brother was again allowed to visit her in jail, but he was not allowed physical contact. With the federal indictment on espionage charges in addition to the wartime censorship violations, she was facing death by electrocution.

However, United States Attorney McNally wasn't convinced if they could persuade a jury that she, and not her husband, had been a Japanese agent. In addition, most of the evidence was circumstantial at best, and could not be introduced in open court without endangering national security. The possibility of this defense creating a reasonable doubt was sufficiently great to therefore warrant the acceptance of the plea of guilty to the lesser crime. The charges of espionage would be dropped.

ꕤ

Chapter 6

The Trial

By July, the defendant—already described as "The War's Number One Woman Spy"—had changed from petulant and defiant to willing to accept a deal. On July 28, 1944, an agreement was reached between U.S. Attorney McNally and Velvalee's attorney, Maurice L. Shane, whereby the espionage and Registration Act indictments were dismissed by Judge Stephen S. Chandler, Jr., assigned to the New York case temporarily from his own district in Oklahoma. Arriving at the Federal Courthouse wearing a black dress and black gloves, Velvalee pleaded guilty to the lesser charge of censorship violation and, hoping to get a lighter sentence, promised to furnish information in her possession concerning Japanese intelligence activities.

The proceeding was brief. Prosecutor McNally announced that the defendant wished to change her not guilty plea to that of guilty, and Maurice Shaine, the defense lawyer assigned by the court, explained that "Mrs. Dickinson had reached this decision herself, and with his approval and that of Aaron Samuelson, also assigned" by the court. August 14 was the date set for sentencing.

Velvalee was described in the *New York Times* as appearing more nervous than on other occasions. "Gone was the tense, defiant manner in which she had demanded, 'Who are all these people?' when she found Federal Bureau of Investigation agents, prosecutors, spectators, clerks, and reporters present at her first arraignment. And though she twisted a handkerchief in black-gloved hands held behind her back, she seemed somehow more relaxed and perhaps resigned to her predicament." When the prosecutor spoke, "She even yawned, decorously behind a hand," the *Washington Times-Herald* reported.

By her admission of guilt to the censorship charges, and now with the charge of espionage dropped, Velvalee no longer faced the death penalty.

Explaining his action, which involved Judge Chandler's dismissal of the espionage indictment, Mr. McNally said:

> *The proof against the defendant was highly circumstantial in nature. In the absence of her confederates now in Japan, in my judgment the defense to be offered by the defendant was to have been that the letters were written by her husband, Lee, who died March 29, 1943.*

Following her guilty plea, with no further need for keeping secret the evidence against Velvalee, United States Attorney McNally immediately made public the letter—the "Springfield letter" as the first intercepted letter was called—that had led to the apprehension of the doll dealer and other details of the case:

> *Dear Friend,*
>
> *You probably wonder what has become of me as I haven't written to you for so long. We have had a pretty bad month or so. My little nephew the one I adore so has a malignant tomer on the brain and isn't expected to live so we are all so crushed that we don't know what we are doing. They are giving him exray on the head and they hope to check it but give us absolutely no hope in a complete cure and maybe not even any relief. I am completely crushed.*

You asked me to tell you about my collection a month ago I had to give a talk to an Art Club so I talked about my dolls and figurines. The only new dolls I have are THREE LOVELY IRISH dolls. One of these three dolls is an old Fisherman with a Net over his back another is an old woman with wood on her back and the third is a little boy.

Everyone seemed to enjoy my talk. I can only think of our sick boy these days.

You wrote me that you had sent a letter to Mr. Shaw, well I went to see MR. SHAW he destroyed YOUR letter, you know he has been ill. His car was damaged but is being repaired now. I saw a few of his family about. They all say Mr. Shaw will be back to work soon.

I do hope my letter is not too sad. There is not much I can write you about these days.

I came on this short trip for mother for business before I try to make out her income report. That is also Why I am learning to type.

Everyone seems busy these days the streets are full of people.

Remember me to your family sorry I haven't written to you for so long.

Truly

Mary Wallace.

Mother wanted to go to Louville but due to our worry the Louville plan put out our minds now.

Mrs. Wallace received the returned letter in June 1942. She had a nephew then ill of an incurable brain ailment. The previous November she had indeed lectured to an art club in Springfield. She even had three dolls that met the descriptions in the letter, although they were not Irish dolls. But she had not sent the letter, and had not been in New York when it was mailed.

Mr. McNally explained that he had been prepared to prove what was the real purpose of the letter—the message intended for the Imperial Japanese Government. The "new" dolls, he said, were warships newly operating in the Pacific—an aircraft carrier draped with safety nets, a warship with wooden superstructure, and the "little boy" was a destroyer.

Mr. Shaw who "distroyed" what it had received from Mrs. Dickinson's Japanese friends, according to Mr. McNally's interpretation, was the USS *Shaw*, the destroyer whose bow was bombed at Pearl Harbor. This destroyer had been fitted with a temporary bow in Honolulu and made the run to San Francisco, arriving there February 16, 1942, where a permanent bow was installed.

Mrs. Dickinson was on the West Coast from January 23, 1942, until she returned in New York on March 1, the day the letter was mailed. It had been written on February 22.

The postscript, Mr. McNally said, referred to the fact that Mrs. Dickinson had been unable to obtain requested information concerning the cruiser USS *Louisville*, which was at sea during the entire month of February, 1942, and thus unavailable to landlocked spies.

Mrs. Wallace had not made a business trip for her mother, nor did she plan to make out her mother's income tax, and she was not learning to use a typewriter. She did know Mrs. Dickinson, and had visited her doll shop at 718 Madison Avenue while in New York, and she had mentioned her nephew's illness to her in a letter.

Mary Wallace had not associated the mysterious letter from Argentina with the tiny, sharp-eyed woman who collected and sold dolls in New York City. But the FBI achieved that, and took possession of the portable typewriter on which Mr. McNally said the letter had been written.

FBI agents made an attempt to re-interview Velvalee on August 9, 1944. However, after her arrival at the United States Court House and prior to the interview, she complained of chest pains to the United States Marshal, saying she was suffering from a serious heart attack. She was returned to the Women's House of Detention where Ruth Collins, superintendent of the Women's House of Detention, ascertained that Velvalee upon arrival indicated no heart condition and was described as being "in excellent spirits."

Federal Judge John McDuffie, two days later, denied a motion presented by Velvalee's attorneys which would permit her to undergo a physical examination by a private physician. This decision came after Assistant United States Attorney Wallace advised the judge that doctors who had examined Velvalee at the Women's House of Detention could find no trace of a heart ailment or any other malady, and that Velvalee had gained 25 pounds since January 21, 1944.

On August 10, 11, and 12, 1944, in a spirit of cooperation, Velvalee admitted to FBI agents that she had prepared and typed the five letters addressed to the individual in Argentina, and that she had used correspondence received by her from her customers to forge their signatures. In the presence of Special Agent Charles F. Lanman, she then prepared in her own handwriting her analysis of the true meaning of the five letters.

She claimed that the information incorporated in her letters was obtained from personal observation and through questioning innocent and unsuspecting citizens in the Seattle area around the Bremerton Navy Yard (the Puget Sound Naval Shipyard), and the Mare Island Navy Yard in San Francisco, something known within the FBI as "bumping" targets who were unaware of what was taking place.

At the peak of World War II, the Bremerton area was home to an estimated eighty thousand residents due to the heavy workload of shipbuilding, repair and maintenance required for the Pacific war effort. As the only shipyard on the West Coast with the capacity to handle aircraft carriers and battleships, its primary effort was the repair of battle damage to ships of the U.S. fleet and those of its allies.

Immediately following the Japanese attack on Pearl Harbor (December 7, 1941), that Monday, December 8, the U.S. Congress declared war on Japan. Five of the six battleships that hadn't been destroyed in the bombing were sent to the Bremerton-Puget Sound Shipyard for modifications and repair: USS *Tennessee* (BB-43), USS *Maryland* (BB-46), USS *Nevada* (BB-36), USS *California* (BB-44), and USS *West Virginia* (BB-48). These battleships were dubbed the "Pearl Harbor Ghosts" because the Japanese had declared them sunk.

In order to prevent any unauthorized surface or submerged boat traffic in local waters, Puget Sound Navy Yard workers stretched an open mesh weave of steel cable across Rich Passage from Bainbridge Island to Orchard Point—the entrance into the shipyard. According to *Nipsic to Nimitz, a Centennial History of Puget Sound Naval Shipyard*, "Two barges provided a double gateway to all passage of authorized vessels. The ferry would approach, give the signal, be recognized and the first gate opened by slacking off the line supporting it between the two barges. The ferry entered the space between the barges, and the gate was closed behind it. Then the second gate opened, and the ferry proceeded on to Bremerton."

The Mare Island Naval Shipyard (MINSY), located just 25 miles northeast of San Francisco in Vallejo, California, made a name for itself as the premier U.S. West Coast submarine port as well as serving as the controlling force in San Francisco Bay Area shipbuilding efforts during World War II. Base facilities included a hospital, ammunition depot, paint and rubber testing laboratories, and schools for firefighters, opticians, and anti-submarine attack during World War II. MINSY reached peak capacity for shipbuilding, repair, overhaul, and maintenance of many different kinds of seagoing vessels including both surface combatants and submarines, and up to fifty thousand workers were employed.

Both the Puget Sound Naval Shipyard and the Mare Island Naval Shipyard provided ample opportunity for an educated, sophisticated, attractive woman who collected dolls and had a keen interest in current affairs to gather vital information. Velvalee was a renowned Manhattan doll expert who traveled the country showing her dolls in the homes of carefully selected clients. Many of these clients tended to be the wives of well-placed officers on the U.S. Navy vessels in the South Pacific. Over tea and doll talk, Dickinson would casually gather information on ship placements and conditions, crucial details that she would relay to her Japanese Government employers via coded letters that discussed the destroyers as if they were dolls.

During her interviews with FBI agents and U.S. Attorney McNally, Velvalee stated that the letters she wrote at her husband's instructions transmitted information about aircraft carriers and battleships damaged at Pearl Harbor, and that names of the dolls appearing in the letters referred to those types of vessels. The personal information in the letters had been taken from the correspondence she received from the women she did business with—other doll collectors.

Velvalee revealed during an interview with the FBI agents that she had destroyed the paper which had the written "code" immediately following her husband's death. She stated that she did not examine the code too closely, but from her recollection she remembered that "it was simple with the primary purpose to transmit to the Japanese government information relating to Allied aircraft carriers and battleships." She also recalled that the letter "C" in Catherine, "E" in Elizabeth, and "M" in Mary Wallace designated geographic locations on the West Coast. For example, the name of Catherine indicated that the information in the letter was obtained in and around the northwest portion of the West Coast; whereas, Elizabeth referred to the central portion; and Mary to the southern. The names of dolls reflected in the letters referred to either carriers or battleships. Where a dislike of a certain doll was expressed, according to Velvalee, it referred to the fact that this particular ship was damaged and undergoing repairs. Where fondness was expressed, hidden reference was made to a vessel under construction or reconversion. In addition, there were statements made apart from those with espionage value that were meant to balance and make the letter readable to otherwise divert suspicion.

When asked to describe the "code" and its physical appearance, she said it was on a piece of paper about eight inches by three and one-half inches. The woman's name—Señora Ines Lopez de Molinali—was written across the long end, and "the so-called code was written this way" (indicating vertically). The code was written only on one side, and the paper had been folded. "If there was information about the Western hemisphere, then any country in the west, such as Ireland would be used; or if the information pertained to the Eastern hemisphere, a country such as China would be used," she explained.

However, even though Velvalee admitted typing the letters and signing them with her customers' names, she denied knowing what the contents meant, and said her involvement was based entirely on money, implying she wasn't an enemy of the United States Government. When the agents pointed out to her the various inconsistencies and contradictory statements she had made in the different interviews, she reverted to denials, inability to remember, or the fact that the information was possessed by her husband only. Rather, she was a struggling widow trying to survive after the exorbitant medical expenses resulting from her husband's long illness and eventual death. "I was so certain I wouldn't be arrested," she stated, believing that using customers' names was a sure trick that wouldn't be discovered, and that her secret "doll code" was untranslatable.

She insisted that her husband, now deceased, had been the real spy and had accepted $25,000 in $100 bills, along with codes and instructions on how to use them, from the Japanese Naval Attaché Ichiro Yokoyama on or about November 26, 1941, at her doll store at 718 Madison Avenue in exchange for providing information to the Japanese. And, she maintained that she had found the money in her husband's bed immediately after his death. In fact, she stressed the fact that she had shut the bedroom door and searched for the money, afraid that the maid or doctor, or relatives would find it and take it.

Unfortunately for Velvalee, none of her protestations helped her case. Blaming her late husband for her predicament created little sympathy for her. Her statements that she had been so sure she would never get caught and that the code she had used was untranslatable made it appear that she only regretted getting caught, but nothing else.

FBI Special Agent L. Vernon Ewing, cryptographer Charles Appel, and Lieutenant Commander Kelso Daly of the Office of Naval Intelligence appeared as witnesses presenting the government's case. One hundred twenty-five potential jurors were vetted for the trial, and one hundred nine exhibits were offered into evidence.

Investigators disclosed that while Velvalee knew the Japanese Naval attaché well, her husband didn't know him at all. In addition, a medical examination had been conducted on Lee Dickerson at the same time he was to have received the payment, and the results of that examination revealed he had serious mental impairment along with his deteriorating heart condition. As far as the money being hidden in his bed, the Dickinsons' maid and nurse both testified that no money was ever concealed there.

Velvalee's love for her husband was also questioned when evidence was introduced about her relationship with Burnell S. Merritt, Western Traffic Manager, Great Northern Railway Company, Seattle, Washington. Even though she denied anything other than a friendship between them, and that he had assisted her and her husband in their travels on the West Coast whenever they used the train, FBI audio recordings indicated otherwise. Particularly damaging were the recordings of Velvalee visiting Merritt's room at the Olympic Hotel just days after her husband had died, and while apparently sitting on Merritt's lap, the conversations that took place between them. In an emotional, hysterical outburst, Velvalee emphatically denied any type of relationship with Merritt other than what she had already told the FBI agents.

Burnell Merritt, when interviewed by FBI agents, recalled that while the Dickinsons were living at the Whitcomb Hotel in San Francisco, he at no time ever heard either of them mention their association or contact with any Japanese individual. More recently, he received a telephone call from Oswald Blucher. Since Merritt did not know the purpose of the telephone call, he did not accept it. A short time later, he received communications from both Oswald and Velvalee requesting that he contribute toward a fund being raised to establish sufficient monies for Velvalee's release on bond. However, he did not answer either of these communications and destroyed them, feeling that if the FBI had her in custody that "she apparently must be pretty well involved; otherwise she would not be in jail."

Evidence also surfaced that Velvalee's doll business and her so-called knowledge and expertise of dolls had been nothing but a front for her illegal activities designed to betray the government of the United States. On one of her trips to California, she was invited to visit a garden party at the home of Mrs. Gustav Mox in order to view the extensive Mox doll collection. The collection filled a small cottage on the mountain side in a Santa Monica setting behind Mrs. Mox's home.

The granddaughter of Mrs. Mox was filled with anticipation and especially excited to show off her grand collection of the many fine French dolls in their collection to this notable expert from New York. When Velvalee saw the dolls, however, dressed as various queens with costumes of hand-embroidered satin gowns, royal purple capes trimmed in ermine tails, and adorned with beautiful jewels, she was overheard saying, "Oh, you collect those?

No one in the East would have them. We have a whole cellar full of them and you can have them for a song." Bonnie Jean Mox, the granddaughter, promptly burst into tears, devastated that the so-called country's leading authority on dolls had dismissed her much-loved collection so out of hand.

The embarrassing incident was compounded when Velvalee, apparently unaware of the distress she had caused the young girl, turned her attention to a large case of Parians, Chinas and Bisque, exclaiming, "Now these are the kinds of dolls we love," completely missing the fact that they were Emma Clear reproductions. Authentic Emma Clear dolls were on display in another case right next to it, which Velvalee ignored or simply didn't notice.

On the same visit, Velvalee was taken to see another collection in which she promptly misidentified as "some more Clear dolls," even though they were a group of fine authentic old ceramics. Other equally revealing faux pas in her dolling days made the more astute collectors question Velvalee's knowledge and speculate that she was not the clever judge of dolls as she claimed to be.

Velvalee's trial originally had been slated for the first week in June 1944, but was postponed due to the excitement surrounding the D-Day invasion of Europe. The new trial was rescheduled for July. It was the first case of an American woman for whom the death penalty had been proposed for espionage. She wore the same clothes as when she was arrested, a brown skirt and brown tweed coat, and a blue hat. It was reported in newspapers that she appeared pale and apathetic.

The qualifications and suitability of the jurors selected had been determined by interviewing 125 "petit jurors" using the Credit Bureau of Greater New York, local draft boards, local police departments, voting records, and the files of the New York Field Division. The forty-six FBI agents assigned the task were instructed that the investigation be limited to file checks and public and semipublic sources. There were to be no interviews of the potential jurors' neighbors or other persons.

Velvalee's lawyer focused everything on the time factor, hoping to get a postponement. By delaying the trial until the end of the war when emotions weren't running so high, his client stood a better chance of the court showing leniency. He, therefore, declared that his client was seriously ill during her stay in prison. But the court found that the health of the defendant was good and that, in reality, she had gained several pounds during the six months she had been incarcerated.

In his one-count indictment, the charge of espionage no longer on the table, United States Attorney James B.M. McNally revealed how the doll shop had functioned as an excellent spy field. In pointing out the activities of Velvalee, he said:

> *The defendant denies that she was a Japanese agent. While professing a great love and devotion for her husband, Lee Taylor Dickinson, she brands him as the traitor. He can't defend his good name, but I can. There is evidence in existence which proves beyond peradventure of doubt that Velvalee was a hired Japanese spy.*

He detailed the defendant's reports with Japanese naval officers and explained the four letters in which the dolls served as secret code.

> *When the Japanese hired her, they were hiring an old friend. It was Velvalee, and not Lee Dickinson, who admits forging her cstomers' names to these letters. I charge that at least ten days before Pearl Harbor she had definite information that the Japanese were planning to go to war with this country.*

> *At least ten days before Pearl Harbor she was hired to get information which, except for the outbreak of the war, the Japanese could have obtained for themselves. What this defendant did was unspeakably foul. It is so horrible that one finds it difficult to believe that a native-born American, no matter how degraded and low, could be guilty of such acts.*
>
> *The dolls talked, said the prosecutor, but we finally managed to understand their language.*

On August 14, 1944, Velvalee Dickinson appeared in court for sentencing dressed in black except for white knit gloves, and now weighing just 90 pounds. In response to a question of the court if she had anything to say before sentence, a weeping Velvalee asked for mercy and pleaded for leniency, claiming once again that she was not a Japanese agent, but rather, Lee, her late husband, had been the actual spy. Breaking down in court, she swore that she didn't know a "battleship from any other ship except that it's larger." She pleaded for a postponement of her sentence for a month on the grounds that she was aiding the Federal Bureau of Investigation.

In his request that the court penalize Mrs. Dickinson to the full limit of the law, United States Attorney James B.M. McNally denied that Velvalee gave

FBI agents valuable information and said the agents had discovered their own evidence. "It is only by most fortuitous circumstances that little, if any, reached its destination."

Velvalee's plea fell on deaf ears as Federal Judge Shackelford Miller, Jr. commented, noting the fact that Velvalee had been born on American soil (*jus soli*) whose parents were both American citizens at the time of her birth (*jus sanguini*):

> *It is hard to believe that some people do not realize that our country is engaged in a life and death struggle. Any help given to the enemy means the death of American boys who are fighting for our national security. You, as a natural-born citizen, having a university education, and selling out to the Japanese, were certainly engaged in espionage. I think that you have been given every consideration by the Government. The indictment to which you have pleaded guilty is a serious matter. It borders close to treason. You were fortunate that the Government did not have you tried on espionage charges. The penalty for such a conviction would have been death or life imprisonment. I, therefore, sentence you to the maximum penalty provided by the law, which is ten years and $10,000 fine.*

After Judge Miller sentenced Velvalee Dickinson, the government revealed that it had intercepted four more letters written by her. These were the returned letters in which Velvalee had used her clients' names and addresses for sending coded messages to her Japanese contact in Argentina.

Still maintaining her innocence and contending that her deceased husband, and not she, was the real traitor to her country, Velvalee was removed immediately to the Federal Correctional Institution for Women at Alderson, West Virginia. On September 5, 1944, in an interview with FBI agents and her attorney, Richard J. Mallin, Velvalee made a request that she be released from prison for two months in order that she could take a much-needed rest and also in order that she could take a course in Spanish so that she might be able to intelligently converse with Spanish-speaking people. It was her desire to assist the government, even "at the risk of my life," in order to obtain the true facts in the case. She also suggested that she be permitted to go directly to South America. This interview was concluded immediately when Velvalee also stated that she had no further information to give in the case other than that which she had already furnished to the government.

With the "Doll Woman" case now over, the conviction won, newspapers continued to carry the story, fueling the curiosity of readers as they imagined that Velvalee's dolls had turned on her and had indeed "talked," thus ultimately creating her downfall. Not only that, she had also been betrayed by the Imperial Japanese Government who switched agents in Buenos Aires without bothering to tell Velvalee.

The FBI informed the press of its heroism, feeding the dramatic details of "the War's No. One Woman Spy" to reporters. When asked by a reporter what made her become a Japanese spy, one FBI agent who had questioned her suggested that "she was an introvert, embittered by life, the frustration of childlessness." The American people simply couldn't get enough of the "Doll Woman" spy.

Most of the newspaper coverage reported that the doll code had been cracked by FBI cryptographers or "a check with the Navy." Hoover himself wrote about the "Doll Woman" in *The American Magazine,* calling her "one of the cleverest woman operators I have encountered. Cultured, businesslike, cunning, and, despite her 50 years of age, most attractive, she presented one of the most difficult problems in detection the FBI has tackled in this war."

C.A. Appel of the FBI Technical Laboratory who first broke the coded letters and Special Agent L. Vernon Ewing were granted recognition for outstanding work in this case.

Elizebeth Friedman, just as she had all through the proceedings, stayed out of the public eye. And while the public learned of the "Doll Woman's" treachery from Hoover, the woman who had analyzed the "Doll Woman's" letters in her spare time, offering up invaluable information to the solving of the case that resulted in a guilty verdict, returned to her primary task of hunting for Nazi spies for the U.S. Army's Cryptoanalysis Bureau. Little more than a footnote in the case involving "the War's No. One Woman Spy," Elizebeth Smith Friedman died in 1980 in Plainfield, New Jersey, at the age of 88.

Chapter 7

The Time Served

In the early 1920's the need for prison reform grew out of concerns of imprisoned activists in the Women's Suffrage movement who experienced harsh prison conditions and cruel treatment for acts of civil disobedience. These women came forward to speak of the indignities and abuse they endured when held as captives in men's prisons. The founding vision was for a "community of women working together under the guidance of other women."

Alderson prison was the culmination of the vision and work of women in twenty-two national organizations. The American Association of University Women, the

National Federation of Business and Professional Women's Clubs, the American Federation of Teachers, the Daughters of the American Revolution, the League of Women Voters, the Republican and Democratic National Committees, and the National Women's Christian Temperance Union were among them. Also supporting the movement was Eleanor Roosevelt, President Franklin D. Roosevelt's wife. These prison reformers sought to protect women inmates from the exploitation of male inmates and staff and to provide a homelike communal setting with provisions for nurseries and childcare to mothers sentenced to prison.

Located about a five-hour driving distance from Washington, DC, Alderson's beautifully landscaped prison included residential cottages named after social reformers, such as Elizabeth Frye—an English prison and social reformer, Jane Addams—a pioneer American settlement activist/reformer, and Mary McLeod Bethune—an American civil rights activist best known for starting a private school for African-American students in Daytona Beach, Florida.

Dr. Mary B. Harris, the prison's first superintendent, held a doctorate in Sanskrit from the University of Chicago. She believed that women prisoners, when treated with dignity and provided with educational opportunities, could "build within themselves a well of self-respect" and learn the skills that would enable them to earn their own living "without dependence on a man or the community."

Serving as a model for prison reform at the time, Alderson was styled after a boarding school environment offering education with no armed guards and no barbed-wire fenced grounds. The prison consisted of primarily work-oriented facilities designed for minor federal offenders. It originally consisted of fourteen cottages built in a horseshoe pattern on two-tiered slopes—the "cottage plan."

The offenders were segregated by race in the cottages, and each building contained a kitchen and rooms for about thirty women. The vast majority of the women were imprisoned for drug and alcohol charges (the "moonshine ladies" from the hills of West Virginia) imposed during the Prohibition era.

A few, like Velvalee, however, were serving time for more serious crimes.

Today, the 159-acre facility is the largest employer in the Alderson, West Virginia, area. While there is still no barbed wire on the fence surrounding the camp, the prisoners have schedules and each one must work. Inmates get holidays off except those who work in the powerhouse and kitchen. They sleep in bunk beds in two large dormitories, and each dormitory holds five hundred-plus inmates. Inmates sleep in a 5-by-9-foot cinderblock cube inside of the open dormitory.

From its beginning, Alderson's staff members have maintained a focus on vocational training and personal growth experiences, with craft-shop activities such as sewing, knitting, landscaping, baking, and basket-weaving an integral part of vocational training. Free time is spent walking around the sidewalk that is set between the two dorms as this is within bounds for the inmates. They also play recreational activities such as volleyball.

The reasons for their imprisonment naturally vary with each inmate. Many, including female inmates transferred from other prisons, are in the drug program offered at Alderson. Most of the inmates have been convicted of non-violent or white-collar crimes. Recently, Martha Stewart, an American retail executive businesswoman, writer, and television personality best known for her cooking and home decorating shows, served a five-month term in the college campus-like environment for lying to investigators about a stock sale. Dubbed as "Camp Cupcake" by the press, Martha preferred to call it "Yale."

When Velvalee was there, however, things were different. Inmates serving time with her included Lilly Stein, who was a Nazi German spy; American jazz singer and song writer Billie Holiday, serving time for the possession of narcotics; Mildred Gillars, an American known as "Axis Sally" who supplied propaganda radio broadcasts for Nazi Germany; Kathryn Kelly, the moll and dynamic force behind gangster "Machine Gun Kelly; and Iva Toguri D'Aquino, known as "Tokyo Rose," an American citizen who participated in English-language propaganda broadcasts transmitted by Radio Tokyo during World War II to Allied soldiers in the South Pacific.

During the 1950s when Velvalee was serving her time, the Kennedy name was relatively unknown, especially in rural West Virginia and an all-female community called Alderson Federal Prison Camp for Women. It had been a decade since Joe Kennedy was the U.S. Ambassador to the Court of Saint James in the United Kingdom. It would be two more years before John

Fitzgerald Kennedy would run for the U.S. Senate, and still another decade after that before he would be elected President of the United States.

At Alderson, the celebrities were more likely to be the inmates themselves, women whose names had appeared regularly in the nation's newspapers as interested readers followed their stories of crime. Some of these names were also noted in Eunice Kennedy Shriver's diary and notebooks. Eunice shared the philosophy on which Alderson was founded—to provide educational opportunities to the inmates so they could "build within themselves a well of self-respect" and learn the skills that would enable them to earn their own living "without dependence on a man or the community."

Educated at the Convent of The Sacred Heart, Roehampton, London, and at Manhattanville College in Upper Manhattan, Eunice Kennedy graduated from Stanford University with a bachelor of science degree in sociology in 1943. Following graduation, she worked for the Special War Problems Division of the U.S. State Department. She eventually moved to the U.S. Justice Department as executive secretary for a project dealing with juvenile delinquency.

In January 1950, Eunice arrived at Alderson Federal Prison Camp for Women for a six-week stay in order to research the needs of incarcerated women with an eye toward helping them transition back into society as responsible citizens. Ethel Shakel Kennedy, Eunice's roommate at Manhattanville College and later, wife of Eunice's brother, Robert Kennedy, believed Eunice had been asked by the Justice Department to go to Alderson under cover and gather information about illegal activities there. "There was something amiss there," she is reported to have said. However, there is no evidence to substantiate that claim.

Rather, Eunice's long-standing interest in the social causes of criminal activity seemed to be her motivating reason for going to Alderson. She stayed with the new warden, Nina Kinsella, who had started her career with the Massachusetts Department of Corrections.

Eunice wrote regularly to her father about the inmates and her thoughts on how best to help them. Concerned that without transitional assistance, that period of time immediately following their release back into society, the women would lapse again into criminal behavior, "Most of the girls have nobody," she wrote. "They haven't committed crimes because they want to be evil, rather because they haven't learned acceptable social ways of behavior." They needed sponsors, but the initial overtures to women's service groups requesting assistance produced discouraging results.

Her emphasis on the dignity of women was driven, in part, by the number of inmates at Alderson whose illegal activities had been perpetrated in conjunction with, or at the urging of, husbands or boyfriends. She believed in the capacity of these women to succeed in spite of the control men exerted over them. "You are free and I am free to do what we want with ourselves and our lives," she told the inmates.

When Eunice left Alderson, she went to Washington trying to line up jobs and mentors for women soon to be released from the prison. The result was, she was able to get a commitment from the president of the United Garment Workers of America to hire qualified seamstresses out of Alderson in factories near their hometowns.

She also had meetings in Boston, New York, Washington, and Chicago with women's clubs to generate more interest among educated women in mentoring the inmates. A short time later she moved to Chicago at the request of Monsignor Vincent W. Cooke, the head of Catholic Charities in Chicago, to work as a volunteer with the House of the Good Shepherd and the Chicago Juvenile Court.

While staying at Alderson, Eunice seemed to be especially drawn to the women charged with war crimes and treason. Iva Toguri D'Aquino worked in Alderson's medical clinic. When Eunice met her, she commented that the quiet and polite Tokyo Rose "will do anything. No job is too menial for her here (Alderson)."

A Los Angeles native whose parents were Japanese immigrants, Iva had been raised as a Christian. She began grammar schools in Mexico and San Diego before returning to Los Angeles with her family to complete high school and eventually graduate from the University of California, Los Angeles, in 1940 with a degree in zoology.

Iva had traveled to Japan to visit an ailing relative just prior to Japan's attack on Pearl Harbor. Unable to return to the United States, she was pressured by the Japanese government to renounce her U.S. citizenship. When she refused, she was declared an enemy alien.

Iva was known to Allied troops in the Pacific as "Tokyo Rose," the name given to a group of unconnected or unrelated women who did radio broadcasts for the Imperial Japanese Government. However, she never used that name on the air, choosing instead the name "Anne" and later "Orphan Ann," and her broadcasts were based on comedy and music rather than anti-American propaganda.

Because she participated in English-language radio broadcasts transmitted by Radio Tokyo to Allied soldiers in the South Pacific during World War II, Iva had been convicted on one vague, unsubstantiated charge of treason—"That on a day during October, 1944, the exact date being to the Grand Jurors unknown, said defendant, at Tokyo, Japan, in a broadcasting studio of The Broadcasting Corporation of Japan, did speak into a microphone concerning the loss of ships." Iva was sentenced to serve ten years at Alderson and pay a $10,000 fine.

After serving six years and two months, she was released January 28, 1956, and moved to Chicago. Later investigations found her radio program, *The Zero Hour,* innocuous, and, to complicate matters for the government, two of the witnesses who testified for the prosecution admitted that their grand jury testimony was perjured. In

1976, President Gerald Ford wrote an executive pardon, full and unconditional, for Iva Toguri D'Aquino which restored her U.S. citizenship.

On January 15, 2006, the World War II Veterans Committee awarded Toguri its annual Edward J. Herlihy Citizenship Award, citing "her indomitable spirit, love of country, and the example of courage she has given her fellow Americans." Toguri died of natural causes in a Chicago hospital on September 26, 2006, at the age of 90.

Similarly, Mildred Elizabeth Gillars, of Portland, Maine, attended Ohio Wesleyan College where she studied drama. In 1934, she moved to Dresden, Germany, to study music, and was later employed as a teacher of English at the Berlitz School of Languages in Berlin.

She became engaged to Paul Karlson who was a naturalized German citizen, and began working as an announcer with the Reichs-Rundfunk-Gesellschaft (RRG), German State Radio. In 1941 when the U.S. State Department was advising nationals to return home, Mildred elected to stay in Germany with her fiancé.

On December 7, 1941, when Pearl Harbor was attacked, things rapidly changed for Mildred. Her fiancé had been killed in action on the Eastern front, and as an American citizen, she was now faced with the prospect of joblessness or prison. Under pressure and afraid, Mildred agreed to a written oath of allegiance to Germany.

When she returned to work, her duties were initially limited to announcing records and participating in chat shows. In 1942, however, Max Otto Koischwitz, the program director in the USA Zone at the RRH, cast Mildred in a new show called *Home Sweet Home.*

No longer apolitical, Mildred soon acquired several derogatory names amongst her GI audience such as Berlin Bitch, Berlin Babe, Olga, and most notably, Axis Sally. This name probably came when asked on air to describe herself, Mildred had said she was "the Irish type… a real Sally."

Dubbed as Hitler's singing propagandist, Mildred was soon cast in more shows from Berlin like *Midge-at-the-Mike, GI's Letter Box,* and *Medical Reports* between 1942 and 1945, each one designed to demoralize American soldiers and exploit their fears.

Immediately following the war, Mildred was formally arrested in Germany and brought to the United

States where she was indicted on ten counts of treason based on ten of her shows. During the trial, however, two counts were dropped, and on March 10, 1949, a jury convicted Mildred on only one count of treason, based on her broadcast *Vision of Invasion* she made on June 4, 1944, just prior to the Normandy invasion. She was sentenced to ten to thirty years at Alderson and a $10,000 fine.

After serving seventeen years, she was released on June 10, 1961, and went to live in Our Lady of Bethlehem Convent in Columbus, Ohio, where she taught French, German, and music at St. Joseph's Academy. She died of colon cancer on June 25, 1988.

Also serving time at Alderson prison while Eunice was doing her research there was Lilly Barbara Carola Stein. Born in Vienna, Austria, to wealthy and respectable parents in 1914, she was recruited as an intelligence agent by *Abwehr*, the German military intelligence service for the *Reichswehr* (the military organization of Germany) and *Wehrmacht* (the unified armed forces of Nazi Germany). The initial purpose of the *Abwehr* was defense against foreign espionage. To this end, the *Abwehr* gathered domestic and foreign information, most of it in the form of human intelligence.

In 1939, Lilly was sent to New York City as a German agent and opened a dress shop where she recruited other agents for *Abwehr* and acted as a forwarding address, successfully moving letters containing orders or sensitive stolen information to and from Germany for fellow spies. An attractive, buxom brunette, she also frequently targeted men at New York nightclubs, attempting to find ways to blackmail them or otherwise entice them to give up valuable secrets.

Lilly was rounded up in June, 1941, as part of the infamous Duquesne spy ring, the largest espionage case in United States history that ended in convictions. A total of 33 members of a German espionage network headed by Frederick "Fritz" Joubert Duquesne were convicted after a lengthy investigation by the Federal Bureau of Investigation. Of those indicted, nineteen pleaded guilty, including Lilly. The remaining fourteen were brought to jury trial in Federal District Court, Brooklyn, New York, on September 3, 1941; all were found guilty on December 13, 1941. On January 2, 1942, the group was sentenced to serve a total of over three hundred years in prison.

Lilly pleaded guilty, despite her assertion that she was forced into the espionage business because she wasn't purely Aryan—and therefore, by refusing to cooperate, she faced being put in a forced labor camp, deported, or worse when the Nazis took Austria. She received sentences of ten years' and two concurrent years' imprisonment for violations of espionage and registration statutes, time to be served at Alderson. After serving twelve years, she was released and moved to France where she found employment at a luxury resort near Strasbourg. The 1945 film *The House on 92nd Street* was based on the Duquesne Spy Ring saga of 1941.

As intrigued as Eunice was of these three women—Iva Toguri D'Aquino, Mildred Elizabeth Gillars, and Lilly Stein—Eunice was especially drawn to Velvalee Dickinson, now 56 years old and 29 years her senior—the former owner of a prestigious collectable doll shop on Madison Avenue in Manhattan who had been convicted of spying for the Japanese during the war. By the time Eunice met Velvalee, the "Doll Woman" had already been at Alderson a little over four years, spending her time writing letters to her brother, Oswald, and asking him to send her things like "bobbie pins," reading the publication *Cathedral Bulletin,* learning how to play the electric organ, writing magazine articles, and reading books such as *Citidal* by A.J. Cronin and *The Razors Edge* by

Somerset Maughan. She also took care of a yellow male cat "which will soon be a father," she wrote to her brother.

It is ironic that on the very day Velvalee was given the maximum sentence of ten years in prison at Alderson and a $10,000 fine for violation of the censorship laws, J.P. Kennedy, Jr., son of ex-ambassador Joseph Kennedy and Eunice's brother, was killed when a Navy bomber he was piloting exploded in flight. And only a year earlier, in August 1943, another brother, John Fitzgerald Kennedy, had been seriously injured by the Japanese in the Solomon Islands, an injury that caused him chronic back pain for the rest of his life.

Some speculate that Eunice felt sympathetic toward Velvalee because she, like Eunice, had graduated from Stanford University. In fact, by strange coincidence, Velvalee belatedly received her degree the same year that Eunice graduated from Stanford. Or maybe it was because she believed Velvalee's story that it had been her husband, Lee, who spied for the Japanese and not her. So many of the women Eunice had met and counselled through her work in social services, after all, had gotten into trouble because of their controlling and manipulative husbands or boyfriends. Or it could have been that Velvalee had worked in social services for a time while living in San Francisco, an interest and passion that Eunice also shared.

Regardless of her reasons, Eunice's actions indicated that she believed the "older" woman deserved a second chance and she, therefore, focused her attention on helping Velvalee. After serving seven years, Velvalee was conditionally and quietly released on April 23, 1951, under the supervision of the federal court system. She would report to the United States Probation Officer, Southern District of New York, until February 13, 1954, at which time, by statute, the "Doll Woman" was no longer of any legal or criminal interest to the United States of America.

Velvalee returned to her home in New York City on West 11th Street and immediately changed her name to "Catherine Dickinson." With the help of Eunice, she was given a job at St. Vincent's Hospital through Eunice's contacts at Catholic Charities in New York City. "I am grateful to you for giving her a chance in spite of her long prison record," Eunice wrote at the time to Monsignor James Lynch, executive director of New York Catholic Charities.

Eunice continued to maintain contact with Velvalee, and in May 1953, Velvalee attended Eunice's wedding to Sargent Shriver in a star-studded Roman Catholic ceremony at Saint Patrick's Cathedral in New York City. Her wedding gift to the couple was monogramed stationary from Tiffany's. Following the ceremony, Velvalee stood in the receiving line at the wedding reception held at the Starlight Roof and the Grand Ballroom of the Waldorf Astoria which featured a fifteen-piece orchestra and an eight-tier wedding cake.

The seventeen hundred guests included such notables as Margaret Truman Daniel, only child of President Harry Truman and First Lady Bess Truman; American financier, Bernard Baruch; Supreme Court Justice William Douglas; Thomas Watson, Jr., the president if IBM; politicians Vincent Impelletteri, mayor of New York City, and Christian Herter, governor of Massachusetts; and Wisconsin senator, Joseph McCarthy.

Less newsworthy but perhaps more conspicuous attending the occasion were former inmates from the Federal Correctional Institution for Women at Alderson, which included Velvalee Dickinson who was now calling herself Catherine Dickinson. Sargent Shriver was overheard quipping to his new father-in-law, Joseph

Kennedy, "I hope you have double guards watching the wedding presents."

A few years later, Velvalee would move to Cape Cod and work as Eunice's administrative assistant. "She was a remarkable secretary," according to Ethel Kennedy, who learned that one of her own treasured childhood dolls, dressed as a Dominican nun, had come from the Velvalee Dickinson doll shop on Madison Avenue.

In September 1963 Eunice tried to secure employment for Velvalee in the United States Pavilion at the following year's New York World's Fair. The position required a "special clearance," however, which prompted an anxious typewritten letter from Velvalee to her mentor. "Will a special clearance be necessary?" she wrote. Even though the conditions of her release from Alderson Correctional Facility had been met nine years earlier, Velvalee worried that the State Department might have a role in hiring and do a background check. "I am certain you realize why I ask this question of you." It turned out that the Department of Commerce was in charge, but it is unclear whether Eunice's efforts got Velvalee a job at the World's Fair dedicated to "Peace through Understanding."

By now Velvalee would have been 70 years old, and she seems to have simply disappeared after that other than a brief mention that she passed away unnoticed in California in 1980.

ჯ ✵ ଓ

Chapter 8

The Aftermath

On the world stage, the Second World War was the biggest event of the 20th century. As many as sixty million people were killed, border lines between countries were erased or altered, cities and towns were reduced to rubble, and families were torn apart as they faced unprecedented hardship and change. The struggle to replace and rebuild would last for generations, and in some instances, goes on even today.

Closer to home the impotent feeling of innocence lost spread across the country and permeated the fabric of democracy. Along with it came the sense of a new reality that life would never be the same. Much has been accomplished since the war years, and yet the effects of "the Big One" continue to be felt not only in the United States, but throughout the world.

There was another stage—this one created by Velvalee and her dolls. It was smaller, but devastating nonetheless. The people she contacted and the places she visited as part of her greed-fueled traitorous scheme were indelibly marked by the actions of the "Doll Woman." In some cases, the consequences of those actions linger still—like the smudge of a fingerprint or the whisper of a ghost.

Velvalee's brother, Oswald Otto (also Ossie) Blucher, married in the 1940s after his sister was sent to Alderson. Maintaining a quiet lifestyle, he died in 1969 in Upper Darby, Pennsylvania, at the age of 66.

The Velvalee Dickinson doll shop at 718 Madison Avenue was eventually sold and for a time housed Beretta Galleries, the flagship store of the Italian arms manufacturer, and hunting sportswear. Today it is the home of Devi Kroell, an exclusive boutique of high-priced fashion designer handbags and shoes. By many, however, it is still remembered as the Velvalee Dickinson doll shop.

The Madison Avenue residence where Velvalee and her husband, Lee, lived in New York before Velvalee moved to West 11th Street following her husband's death was replaced by a sixteen-story brown-brick apartment building known as the Carlton House designed by Kenneth B. Norton in 1950 and used as a women's dormitory for two New York institutions for higher learning. It later came to be called the Helmsley Carlton House. In 2010, the elegant building was acquired from the Helmsley Estate for $170 million by Extell Development and Angelo, Gordon & Co., and was approved by the Landmarks Preservation Commission for its conversion to sixty-eight condominium apartments and one townhouse unit. The conversion was completed in 2013. In its description it is noted that Velvalee Dickinson had once lived there.

Yokoyama Ichiro, Japan's last naval attaché to the United States prior to the war and one of Velvalee's primary contacts, was given command of the *Kuma*, Japanese Imperial Navy general purpose light cruisers, for a year, then made top aide to the Navy minister, where he served the remainder of the war. He had the unpleasant duty of leading the Navy's delegates to Manila to arrange details of the Japanese surrender. He died on July 28, 1993.

Kaname Wakasugi, the Japanese consul general and friend of Velvalee, was reported to have left Washington, D.C. on August 5, 1941, for San Francisco where he then departed aboard Southern Pacific Railroad *Lark* for Los Angeles at 9 p.m. on August 7. On August 15, 1944, he left Los Angeles for Japan aboard the *Asama Maru*, and the FBI no longer tracked his movements after that time.

The ships Velvalee reported on to her Japanese contact, each have their own history.

The USS *Shaw* (DD-373) returned to Pearl Harbor on August 31, 1942, after the repairs on the massive damage inflicted by the Japanese bombing were completed in San Francisco. Also referred to as old *New Orleans,* having come from the U.S. Naval Station New Orleans, Louisiana, on August 23, 1940, *Shaw* escorted convoys between Hawaii and the West Coast for two months. It was then sent on to the South Pacific in October of that year where it participated in the Battle of Santa Cruz and the Guadalcanal Campaign. She continued to serve in the Pacific through the rest of World War II, earning eleven battle stars. USS *Shaw* was decommissioned in October 1945 and sold for scrap in July 1946.

The USS *Louisville* (CA-28) was at sea the entire month of February 1942 when Velvalee was trying to gather information on it to give to the Imperial Japanese Government. *Louisville* continued serving in the South Pacific until the end of the war, and in August 1945 she was assigned post-war duties. Decommissioned on June 17, 1946, *Louisville* then entered the Atlantic Reserve Fleet where she remained for the next thirteen years. *Louisville* was struck from the Naval Vessel Register on March 1, 1959, and sold on September 14 of that same year to the Marlene Blouse Corporation of New York. The USS *Louisville* was awarded thirteen battle stars for her service during World War II.

Louisville's ship's bell is on display at the Navy Operational Support Center in Louisville, Kentucky. One of her main battery 8 inch 55 caliber gun turrets (Turret No. 2) damaged in a kamikaze attack on January 5, 1945, was removed and taken to the Nevada Test Site where it was converted into a rotating radiation detector to collect data on nuclear tests.

The USS *Saratoga* (CV-3), following the attack on Pearl Harbor, became the centerpiece of the unsuccessful American effort to relieve Wake Island and was torpedoed by a Japanese submarine a few weeks later. After lengthy repairs, the ship once again resumed its support of Allied forces throughout the South Pacific.

In mid-1944, the ship became a training ship for the rest of the year and eventually was permanently modified as a training carrier with some of her hangar deck converted into classrooms. *Saratoga* remained in this role for the rest of the war and was then used to ferry troops back to the United States after the Japanese defeat in August 1945 leading up to its surrender on September 2, 1945.

The ship was a target for nuclear weapon tests during Operation Crossroads in 1946. This was a test conducted at Bikini Atoll to evaluate the effect of the atomic bomb on ships. In recent years, the submerged wreck, the top of which is only 50 feet below the surface, has become a scuba diving destination. The USS *Saratoga* received eight battle stars for her service during World War II.

In the late 1930s, an article titled "Dolls Are More Than Toys" appeared in the *American Collector* magazine, a publication which ran from 1933 until 1948 and served antique collectors and dealers. Reprinted by Richmond Huntley in March 2009, the article mentions Velvalee Dickinson as it explains why dolls play such an important role within the world of collecting:

> *Doll groups could well be started by children. In the shop of Velvalee Dickinson, New York City, I overheard this conversation:*
>
> *A young woman had come in to choose some dolls for her little girl. She picked some tiny ones dressed in Norwegian costume, two in Mexican dress, a Chinese mandarin and a Russian soldier. "The world has grown so small," she said. "My little girl will need to get better acquainted with her neighbors."*

That same sentiment could very well have been expressed today. Compare the universal and instant doll market of today with that not-too-distant past. When Velvalee had her shop, specific sought-after dolls were found through correspondence, telephone calls, or visiting doll stores, with searches for a doll often taking months or years.

Today, thanks to eBay, Google search, and other Internet sites, dolls are located or traded anytime and anywhere in an unbelievably liquid market. Online searches for a particular doll of a certain age or unusual provenance can produce results within minutes, no matter who the collectors are or where they are located.

This has had a drastic effect on prices, and it has made it somewhat difficult to determine what the true value of a doll actually is at any given moment. A doll's popularity or rarity as well as its condition can frequently drive its price either up or down. Yet, perhaps because of this, interest in doll collecting still remains popular and desirable.

Still very much a part of this collectors' market is Velvalee Dickinson. Even now, years later, Velvalee's dolls continue to draw attention.

In November 2005, Public Broadcasting Station green-lighted a fourth season of the acclaimed series *History Detectives,* to be broadcast in the summer of 2006. Among the stories to be explored were "Two ornate dolls that might be connected to one of the most notorious spy schemes of WW II in which American Velvalee Dickinson (aka the Doll Woman) sent coded messages through South America to the Japanese."

The story of Lee Lawrence Pierce, who was 13 years old when she first discovered her mysterious Mexican gypsy rag doll in the window of a bookstore that was located next to Velvalee Dickinson's doll shop, continues even today. The doll named "Perla Negra," so named for her eyes of real black Mexican pearls, still hides its secrets.

Over time, its owner, now close to 90, has learned that Perla was purchased at a Mexican flea market by Lee Dickinson who gave it to Velvalee for her collection even though she thought the doll was ugly and didn't even want it. He paid fifteen pesos for it, but it was worth considerably more because of its black pearl eyes.

Lee Lawrence Pierce has tried unsuccessfully for decades to learn whether this somewhat imposing, "scary" doll placed in various poses and positions in the bookstore window was used to signal new information that Velvalee had gathered for Japan. From her childhood memories, she remembers seeing Velvalee quietly talking to a well-dressed Japanese man and telling him that if the Mexican gypsy doll was not in the bookstore window, it was not safe to come to her doll shop.

Perla Negra, a doll that seemed somehow haunted, was an early addition in Lee Lawrence Pierce's collection, the first being a Japanese dancing doll in a glass case that her grandfather had given her. Unable to understand what she interpreted as a look of terror in the doll's eyes, she eventually paid a doll restorer five hundred dollars to "fix" the eyes.

A few years after acquiring Perla Negra, Lee Lawrence Pierce worked as a State Department employee in Buenos Aires first as a secretary, then teaching English to Argentine school children. By a strange coincidence, Pierce lived on the same street in Buenos Aires to which Dickinson mailed her secrets to the Japanese agents. She did not know then, however, of the street's connection to Dickinson.

In April 1951 Pierce was once again living in New York City when the news broke about Velvalee's release from Alderson Correctional Facility. Numerous newspapers covered the story of the "Doll Woman," along with a photograph of Velvalee.

It was the photograph that immediately brought back the memory of a young girl holding a Mexican gypsy doll in the book store, only to have it yanked out of her arms by an angry woman. She recognized Velvalee from the photograph in the newspaper as being the same woman in the bookstore that day. Most hurtful about the memory was how Velvalee roughly carried the doll dangling by its leg as she hastily walked away, her red high-heeled shoes loudly clattering on the hard-wood floor.

It has been Pierce's hope through the years that in solving the secrets held by Perla, it would end her doll's long purgatory as a possible accomplice in treason. It might also explain her own relationship to this sad-looking doll that both allured and terrified her for so many decades.

In her exhaustive, determined search, Lee Lawrence Pierce has collected clues about Perla's former owner, saving stacks of faded papers, the responses to hundreds of queries to the governments of the United States and Japan. Her unfaltering mission has been to find the answers to her questions:

Did Velvalee Dickinson loan Perla Negra to the bookstore owner, Dickinson's neighbor and landlord, with the specific intention of using Perla as a signal doll?

Did the doll's intermittent and changeable positions in the store's front display window mean anything? If so, what?

And, most important of all,

How many people were killed because of Perla?

Just as Velvalee had a Japanese Daruma good luck doll, Perla Negra has been Lee Lawrence Pierce's good luck doll. Today, with close to two hundred dolls in her collection from all corners of the world, Lee Lawrence Pierce's imagination continues to be stirred by Perla Negra and the role she might have played on Velvalee's stage.

Just recently, a doll was put on display at the Warehouse 13 Artifact Database, a doll that had been part of Velvalee's valuable collection and used to conceal hidden messages. Possibly evidence seized by the FBI and used in its investigation against Velvalee, the description of the doll states: "The doll lets the user form hidden messages within or using a physical object. Only the intended recipient will know how to understand it, which is activated by touch. Correspondence by this method is considered nearly airtight, but there is one recurring kink:

Whenever the sender signs his or her name, even electronically, the ink will rearrange itself on the medium to tell secret information the user knows."

Additionally, even now, avid doll collectors eagerly search the Internet, auction houses, and antique store offerings for dolls with the provenance of having come from Velvalee Dickinson's exclusive doll shop on Madison Avenue. These dolls fetch enormous prices not only because of their age, history, and rarity, but because of their association to Velvalee Dickinson, the "Doll Woman" who was the first American woman to face the death penalty on charges of spying for a wartime enemy.

It is significant to note that given the wide-spread fear and paranoia of Japanese espionage in the United States during World War II, and the internment camps, only one person was known to have successfully passed military information to the Imperial Japanese Government following Pearl Harbor: Velvalee Dickinson.

Like her dolls, cloaked in mystery and wrapped in secrets, Velvalee chose what she would do with her life—the decisions she would make, the actions she would take.

And she paid for it.

When she was released from Alderson Correctional Facility, she continued to live a life in secrecy—changing her name and conducting herself in discreet obscurity. Being invisible.

There is no record of Velvalee after 1980 other than she quietly passed away in California. She would have been 87 years old then.

Perhaps she succeeded in becoming unnoticed, so she could live out her life in anonymity. One can imagine her visiting the Nippon Club near Washington Square, traditionally dressed in a "wafuku," the authentic Japanese attire—a beautifully embroidered silk kimono with the long, wide sash or "obi" wrapped around her waist, her feet covered in the "hanao"—the split-toed socks ("tabi") and wooden platform footwear ("geta"), and her hair styled and adorned, looking very much like one of her Japanese dolls—sipping tea in quiet contemplation.

ꕥ ❋ ꕥ ꕥ ❋ ꕥ ꕥ ❋ ꕥ

Photo Credits

Velvalee Dickinson
(Courtesy of FBI)

Alderson, West Virginia, Correctional Institution of Women
(Courtesy of FBI Vault)

Axis Sally
(Courtesy of Ones Media)

Bombing of USS Gunboat Panay (PR-5)
(Courtesy of USSPanay.org)

Doll Used in Transmitting Coded Messages
(Courtesy FBI Vault)

Early English Wax over Wood Dolls in Velvalee's Collection
(Reproduced from *The Dolls of Yesterday*)

Elizebeth Friedman
(Courtesy of Wikipedia)

Eunice Kennedy Shriver
(Courtesy of Eunice Kennedy Shriver.org)

Formerly Velvalee Dickinson's Doll Store, 718 Madison Ave, New York NY
(Courtesy of FBI)

Historic Old Cemetery – Sacramento
(Courtesy of Committee of Sacramento)

J. Edgar Hoover
(Courtesy of FBI)

Lilly Barbara Carola Stein
(Courtesy of FBI)

Mare Island, Naval Shipyard in 1946
(Courtesy of Wikipedia)

Mare Island, Shipyard Drydock
(Courtesy of Mare Island Museum)

O'Higgins Street, Buenos Aires, Argentina
(Courtesy of A.J. Ferraro)

Perla Negra
(Reproduced from *More than Meets the Eye*)

President Franklin D. Roosevelt
(Courtesy of Office of the Historian)

Secretary of State Cordell Hull
(Courtesy of Office of the Historian)

Spanish Gypsy Doll in Velvalee's Collection (Courtesy of Boston Globe)
Special Agent in Charge Robert L. Shivers (Courtesy of FBI)
The Attack on Pearl Harbor
(Courtesy of the National Archives)

The Store Front of Velvalee Dickinson's Doll Store
(Courtesy of the FBI)

Tokyo Rose
(Courtesy of Biography.com)

USS Louisville (CA-28) – 1945
(Courtesy of Naval History and Heritage Command)

USS Louisville (CA-28), at Mare Island during Refitting, New Guns, New Radar and Fire Controller - Aug - Dec 1942

(Courtesy of Wikipedia)

USS Louisville (CA-28), Ship's Bell
(Courtesy of Wikipedia)

USS Panay (PR-5)
(Courtesy of Wartime History)

USS Saratoga (CV-3), Launching Planes, circa Summer 1941
(Courtesy of Wikipedia)
USS Saratoga (CV-3), Aircraft on the Flight Deck, Preparing for Launching, circa
1929-30
(Courtesy of Wikipedia)

USS Shaw (DD-373), Pearl Harbor 7 Dec 41 After Explosion of the Forward Magazine (Courtesy of Naval History and Heritage Command)

USS Shaw (DD-373) - 1942 With New Bow (Courtesy of Naval History and Heritage Command)

USS Shaw (DD-373) Exploding - Pearl Harbor
(Courtesy of Naval History and Heritage Command)

USS Shaw (DD-373), With Temporary Bow (Courtesy of Naval History and Heritage Command)

Velvalee Dickinson
(Courtesy of the FBI)

ꝏ ✵ ꝏ

Bibliography

Books

Hoehling, A.A. *Women who Spied: True Stories of Feminine Espionage.* Lanham, Maryland: Dodd, Mead & Company, 1993.

Kahn, David. *The Code Breakers: The Comprehensive History of Secret Communication from Ancient Times to the Internet.* New York, New York: Scribner, 1996.

Kawashima, Yasuhide. *The Tokyo Rose Case: Treason on Trial.* Lawrence, Kansas: University Press, 2013.

Lucas, Richard. *Axis Sally: The American Voice of Nazi Germany.* Havertown, Pennsylvania: Casemate, 2010.

McNamara, Eileen. *Eunice: The Kennedy Who Changed the World.* New York, New York: Simon & Schuster, 2018.

Pierce, Lee L. *More than Meets the Eye: True Stories of Seven Dolls.* Xlibris.com, 2014.

Roland, Paul. *Nazi Women of the Third Reich.* London, England: Arcturas, 2018.

Singer, Kurt. *The World's 30 Greatest Women Spies.* New York, New York: Wilfred Funk, 1951.

St. George, Eleanor. *The Dolls of Yesterday.* New York, New York: Charles Scribner's Sons, 1948.

U.S. Government Historical Reports on War Administration: *A Report on the Office of Censorship,* Washington, DC: Government Printing Office, 1946.

Newspapers and Periodicals

Albelli, Alfred. "Court Blocks Cell Visitors to Doll Lady," *Daily News,* New York, New York, February 21, 1944.

Albelli, Alfred. "Tax Troubles Increase Woe of Doll Lady," *Daily News,* New York, New York, January 31, 1944.

Armstrong, Pennelope. "Behind a Doll's Mask," *Philadelphia Inquirer,* Philadelphia, Pennsylvania, February 20, 1944.

Bovsun, Maria. "The Doll Woman," *Daily News,* New York, New York, February 20, 2005.

Goldstein, Alvin. "Strange Case of the Talking Dolls," *St. Louis Post-Dispatch,* St. Louis, Missouri, September 3, 1944.

Logan, Ruth. "Hobby Uncovers Miscellany of Odd Knowledge, *Chicago Tribune,* Chicago, Illinois, August 26, 1945.

Love, Herman. "Feats of the FBI: Trapping the Women Spies in Complex Enemy Network," *Philadelphia Inquirer,* Philadelphia, Pennsylvania, March 10, 1946.

Robertson, Stewart. "Dolled-Up Disloyalty," *Dayton Daily News,* Dayton, Ohio, October 1, 1944.

Singer, Kurt. "Valvalee Dickinson, Dangerous Japanese Spy, Operates in a Swank Manhattan Doll Shop," *Des Moines Tribune,* Des Moines, Iowa, August 26, 1952.

Singer, Kurt. "The Lady with the Dolls," *The Evening Sun,* Baltimore, Maryland, August 12, 1952.

"Collector Tries to Decipher Doll's Roll in WWII Spy Network," *Boston Globe,* Boston, Massachusetts, September 11, 2001.

"Dealer in Dolls Guilty of Sending Ship Data Abroad," *St. Louis Post-Dispatch,* St. Louis, Missouri, July 29, 1944.

"Doll Woman Cleared as Spy, Admits Coding," *Daily News,* New York, New York, July 29, 1944.

"Doll Lady Spy Case Bail Set at $25,000," *Daily News,* New York, New York, February 12, 1944.

"Doll Lady Sees Kin Under FBI's Eyes," *Daily News*, New York, New York, February 22, 1944.

"Doll Store Owner Given Stiff Term," *Nevada State Journal,* Rene, Nevada, August 15, 1944.

"Doll Woman Is Sentenced for Assisting Jap Agents," *The Daily Oklahoman,* Oklahoma City, Oklahoma, August 15, 1944.

"FBI Nabs Doll Woman for Code Notes," *Daily News,* New York, New York, January 22, 1944.

"Gets 10 Years for Conspiring with Japanese," *Daily Review,* Hayward, California, August 14, 1944.

"Miss Florence B. Hoblin Is Wed In Crestwood At Her Home," *The Herald Statesman,"* Yonkers, New York, May 3, 1947.

"Mme. Dickinson's Dolls Delivered Her to the FBI," *The San Francisco Examiner,"* San Francisco, California, March 19, 1944.

"Mrs. Velvalee Dickinson," *AP Wireservice,* New York, New York, May 5, 1944.

"Woman Is Given 10-Year Sentence," *The Fresno Bee, The Republican,* Fresno, California, August 14, 1944.

"Woman Aiding Japs Gets 10-Year Term," *Courier-Post,* Camden, New Jersey, August 15, 1944.

"Woman Indicted as Spy," *The Detroit Free Press,* Detroit, Michigan, May 6, 1944.

Internet

Buese, Denise. "Doll Talk, The Story of Velvalee Dickinson, World War II Spy," https://issuu.com/hudsongraphics/docs/a_capital_affair/93, 2013

Facone, Jason. "The Most Awesome Codebreaker in WWII Was a Woman," https://www.wired.com/story/world-war-2-codebreakers-elizebeth-smith-friedman/, December 27, 2017

https://www.fbi.gov/history/famous-cases/velvalee-dickinson-the-doll-woman

https://www.etsy.com/market/velvalee_dickinson

https://www.google.com/maps/@40.7663487,-73.9693875,3a,15y,98.36h,88.25t/data=!3m6!1e1!3m4!1sBuG8l0Z4lT6E8yutiqlJuQ!2e0!7i16384!8i8192

http://warehouse-13-artifact-database.wikia.com/wiki/Velvalee_Dickinson%E2%80%99s_Doll

http://dollsfromtheattic.blogspot.com/2011/06/adelina-patti-last-rose-of-summer-1905.html

https://www.whatisthemeaningofname.com/what-is-the-meaning-of-the-name-velva-7363/#The_Meaning_Of_The_Name_Velva

http://www.newjerseyhills.com/print_only/obituaries/florence-becker-hoblin-flather-former-personal-secretary-to-gen-joseph/article_649c2bd0-8a83-5d11-af36-7181d5554ee1.html

en.wikipedia.org/wiki/Velvalee_Dickinson

www.fbi.gov/.../famous-cases/velvalee-dickinson-the-doll-woman

https://gizmodo.com/the-strange-case-of-the-doll-seller-who-desperately-wan-1709899500

girlspy.wordpress.com/2008/12/13/velvalee-dickinson

wartimespyladies.blogspot.com/2013/11/velvalee-dickinson-1893-1980.

military.wikia.com/wiki/Velvalee_Dickinson

www.smithsonianmag.com/history/spy-doll-shop-180958251

en.metapedia.org/wiki/Velvalee_Dickinson

prezi.com/n2gxgdzax0lx/velvalee-dickinson

infogalactic.com/info/Velvalee_Dickinson

dbpedia.org/page/Velvalee_Dickinson

listverse.com/2014/04/12/10-amazing-female-spies-you-might-not-know

www.findagrave.com/memorial/25154231/elizebeth-friedman

fbistudies.com/resources

military.wikia.com/wiki/Elizebeth_Smith_Friedman

forensicpsych.umwblogs.org/fbi

https://www.bustle.com/articles/3072-5-infamous-women-you-dont-know-about-because-female-criminals-hit-the-glass-ceiling-too

en.wikipedia.org/wiki/Elizebeth_Friedman

www.networkworld.com/.../the-history-of-steganography.html

http://mentalfloss.com/article/502063/retrobituaries-elizebeth-friedman-americas-unsung-wartime-codebreaker

musingswithkimmee.blogspot.com/2015/11/tale-of-american-spy.html

https://blog.adafruit.com/2018/01/01/world-war-iis-best-codebreaker-was-a-woman-womeninstem/

https://calebandlindapirtle.com/the-doll-shop-lady-was-a-spy/

https://www.jihadwatch.org/2018/07/muslim-from-dearborn-captured-on-an-islamic-state-battlefield

https://archives.fbi.gov/archives/news/stories/2008/august/famfaces_080108

www.coursehero.com/file/25231764/CCJS-321-Week-5docx

en.wikipedia.org/wiki/Alderson_Federal_Prison_Camp

www.myheritage.com/names/velvet_dickinson

www.onthisday.com/history/birthdays/october/12

https://www.cityrealty.com/nyc/park-fifth-ave-79th-st/carlton-house-21-east-61st-street/review/4408

https://www.sofmag.com/1942-wwii-intrigue-agent-nd-98-case-of-the-long-island-double-agent-the-case-of-the-treasonous-dolls/

https://mysteryinthehistory.com/doll-woman-a-spy-in-wwii/

https://doll-college.blogspot.com/2014/

https://dirkdeklein.net/category/japanese-americans/

http://pixelpatriot.blogspot.com/2012/

https://twitter.com/NSAGov/status/1030095585108480000

www.collectorsweekly.com/articles/dolls-are-more-than-toys

https://forum.axishistory.com/viewtopic.php?t=225944

http://www.spywriter.com/robots/steganography.html

abuse.wikia.com/wiki/Japanese_American_internment

nationaldollclub.org/aboutusinterestingfacts.html

wwwdollmuseum.blogspot.com/2011/12/of-dolls-and-stamps.html

www.historicoldcitycemetery.org

http://nisei.hawaii.edu/object/06_sue.html

http://nisei.hawaii.edu/object/io_1162881936750.html

www.fbi.gov/services/information-management/foipa

ℵ ❋ ℵ

Index